How to Sell Your Business for the Most Money

Simple Steps You Can Take Today
To Improve the Value and Marketability of Your Business

THIRD EDITION

Grover Rutter CPA, ABV, CVA, BVAL, CBI, CFFA

Disclaimer

This publication is designed to provide accurate and insightful information with regard to the subject matter covered. It is sold with the understanding that the author and publisher are not rendering accounting, legal, valuation or other professional advice for a reader's specific circumstances. If legal, accounting, valuation or other expert assistance are required, the services of competent professionals should be sought.

Copyright 2013, Grover Rutter
All Rights Reserved
ISBN 978-1-304-30083-6

Foreword

If you're like most business owners, you have occasionally wondered *what your business is worth*. Perhaps you have asked your accountant about the value of your business. But do you know that there is a much more important question that you **should** ask first?

IS MY BUSINESS SELLABLE?

That might sound like a silly question, but the reality is this: in my 30 plus years of experience I have observed that *8 out of every 10 businesses are not sellable in their current condition* (or at least salable for a price anywhere near what the owner had anticipated). Ok, you may be thinking that this statement doesn't apply to you and your business. Read on to see what your business might be missing in order to gain the highest possible sale price.

If your business is not ready to go on the market today and garner the best price possible, you may be sadly disappointed with the eventual sales price and terms. Consider this: *what if you needed to sell due to sudden adverse life events such as health issues, accidents, divorce, or "business owner burn out"(BOB)? (Learn more about "BOB" at www.gruttercpas.com)*. These unexpected events can turn you and your family's world upside down.

Two key issues that are universally considered when getting ready to sell are:

- How long will it take to convert my business to cash?, and
- Is my business in the best possible condition to gain the highest price?

There are a variety of issues that can cause your business to be unsellable, and almost all of them can be controlled by relatively simple actions you can immediately take.

In the following pages, we will discuss *Key Value Concepts* and then identify and discuss the *"Value-Killers"* that can cast your business in an unfavorable light, thus reducing its marketability and value, i.e., less cash in your pocket when you sell. You will also find many useful strategies and ideas that can pay big dividends when you sell.

After reading this guide, please take the time to review the checklists in the back section. You will find the information helpful. Also, I direct your attention to numerous articles about selling your business located on our website www.gruttercpas.com. I suggest you read not only the Sellers articles but the articles under the Buyers section as well. It is important to have a good understanding of what a Buyer is looking for as you move towards the process of selling your business.

No matter the size of your business, large or small, this guide has been written to help you improve the *value, marketability and salability* of your business.

Contents

FOREWORD 3

UNDERSTANDING VALUE 8

CASH FLOW: THE ULTIMATE VALUE-DRIVER 11
   What is the Difference between Profit and Cash Flow? 12
   How to Convert Profit to Cash Flow 12
      How to Calculate Your Company's EBITDA 15
   Sellers Discretionary Earnings (SDE) 15
      How to Calculate Your Company's Seller Discretionary Earnings (SDE) 16

HOW MUCH PROFIT SHOULD MY BUSINESS MAKE? 19
   What is Financial Benchmarking? 19
   Hiring a Professional 21
   Do It Yourself Benchmarking 22
      Ten Free Sources of Industry Financial Data 22
      Three Inexpensive Sources of Industry Data 23
      Example *of Peer Financial Benchmark Data for Manufacturers:* 24

IDENTIFYING THE VALUE-KILLERS AND VALUE-BUILDERS 28
   Heavy Reliance on the Owner 31
      The Man Who Did it All 31
      Keys to Success 32
   Lack of Profitability and Cash Flow 33
   Under-Reported Income 34
      Gambling with the Tax Collector 35
      Bad Perception 35
      Unreported Income Cheats the Business Owner 36
      Case History 36
   Overstated Expenses 37
      Detection May be Easy 38
      Know When to Add Back…and When to Amend 39
   Incorrectly Reported Inventory 41
      Incorrect Work in Progress Inventory 41
      Understanding Unbilled Work in Progress 42
      Demonstrating the Differences in Inventory Valuations 43
   Over Stated Inventory 45
      Suggestions for Improvement 46
   Downward Trend in Sales and Profits 47
      What is Trend Analysis? 47
      Percentage of Change 47
      Calculation of Change Example: 48
      The Fly in the Ointment 49
      Nobody Wants to Buy a Grab Bag 50

- Operating Assets vs. Non Operating Assets 50
- Outdated Products and Services 51
  - Buggy Whips and the Commodore 64 53
- Outdated Information and Operating Technologies 54
  - Information Technologies 54
  - Operating Technologies 55
  - Exception to the Rule 56
  - Waiting on the Next Owner 57
- Outdated Bookkeeping/Accounting Systems 58
  - Poorly Prepared Financial Statements 59
- Labor Union Contracts 60
- High Employee Turnover 61
  - What does Employee Turnover Cost? 61
  - The Causes of Turnover 62
- Environmental Issues 63
  - When "Clean" Might be "Dirty" 64
  - All that Shines is not Aluminum! 65
  - What You Can Do 66
- Safety Issues 66
- Regulatory Issues 67
- Customer Concentration Issues 67
  - Can You Hear Me Now? 68
- Industry Concentration Issues 69
- Competitive Pressures 70
  - Good News Travels Fast 70
  - Combating Competitive Pressures 72
- Appearances 73

OTHER IMPORTANT CONSIDERATIONS 74

- Choosing the Wrong Time to Sell 74
- Failing to Hire Experienced Advisors 74
- Consider the Tax Implications of Your Sale 76
- Have Your Company Appraised 77
- Plan in Advance 77

PREPARE FOR BUYER DUE DILIGENCE IN ADVANCE 78

- Preparing for the Process 78
  - Is Your Organization in Good Order? 79
  - Legal Information 79
  - Financial Information 80
  - Physical Assets 81
  - Real Estate 81
  - Intellectual Property 82
  - Employees and Employee Benefits 82
  - Licenses and Permits 83

> Environmental Issues..83
> Taxes 84
> Material Contracts 84
> Product or Service Lines 85
> Customer Information 85
> Litigation 86
> Insurance Coverage 86
> Professionals 87
> Articles and Publicity 87

TACKLE DEAL-KILLERS EARLY ON 88

CONCLUSION 89

PLANNING CHECKLISTS 90
> CHECKLIST: FACTORS THAT INCREASE OR DECREASE THE VALUE OF YOUR BUSINESS 90
> CHECKLIST: DOES YOUR COMPANY HAVE THESE VALUE-DRIVERS? 92
> CHECKLIST: POSSIBLE RISKS ASSOCIATED WITH YOUR BUSINESS 95
> CHECKLIST: 18 POINT SELF ASSESSMENT TOOL 99
> CHECKLIST: MISTAKES FREQUENTLY MADE BY BUSINESS SELLERS 102

ABOUT THE AUTHOR 105

Understanding Value

Before identifying value-killers, I thought it would be helpful to understand the term *value*. Probably one of the most difficult or misunderstood economic questions ever asked is: *"What is value?"*

I turned to my old friend *Google* and asked, *"What is value?"* I was hoping for a host of really brilliant yet simple insights. That didn't quite work out as I had hoped. The outcome of my search included religious, moral, philosophical, and economic discussions. All those discussions were very boring, so I opted to save you the pain of reading them.

A short business definition of *value* is simply this: *"value is the extent of sacrifice a Buyer is willing to make in order to satisfy a particular need for whatever is of importance to the Buyer at that particular point in time."*

Allow me to demonstrate the definition by asking a question. "Which has more value: a barrel full of gold or a barrel full of water?"

To a thirsty person stranded in the desert, the barrel of water will be much more desirable and valuable than the gold. The parched pilgrim might happily exchange the barrel of gold for the water, especially in a life or death situation. On the other hand, that same person, already possessing the necessary shelter, nourishment, and hydration, will place a much higher value on the gold than on the water. In general terms, *value is associated with the time, the place, and the extent of need (or demand).*

The foregoing discussion provides a basic understanding of value for inanimate, tangible, and real property. But the *value of a business* involves many more twists, turns and other considerations.

Let's talk more specifically about business value, and ask this question: "What makes a <u>business</u> valuable?"

Something that adds value to a product or service; an activity or organizational focus that enhances the value of a product or service in the **perception** *of the consumer and which therefore creates value for the producer. Advanced technology, reliability, or reputation for customer relations can all be value-drivers.*

I direct your attention to the bolded word **perception.** Perception is much like beauty; *it is all in the eye of the beholder*. Those attributes of a business that are perceived by the Buyer (marketplace) as beautiful are **value-drivers**. In the mind of the marketplace, they create perceived value.

In his article *Getting Results—What Makes a Business Valuable?*[1] Paul Svendsen wrote the following description of what contributes to business value:

- **Loyal Customers and Employees.** Turnover in customers or employees can cost a business a lot of money and valuable time. Loyal customers represent quality revenue, and loyal employees can create higher levels of customer satisfaction on a consistent basis.
- **Systems.** A business is nothing more than a bundle of processes. The level to which the business is systematized will have a dramatic effect on the marketability of the business. A business that relies on the owner being there all the time, for example, is simply less marketable than a business that can run independently of the owner. The development of systems is critical to creating a business that really works.
- **A Unique Core Differentiator.** Also known as a Unique Selling Proposition, a Unique Core Differentiator (UCD) is a means of differentiating a business from its competitors. Having a UCD means that the business may be less dependent on pricing as a strategy for growing its business. A UCD might be the way a business packages its products or services, or the way it promotes itself in a way its competitors cannot match.
- **Customer Focus.** A business that obtains regular, candid feedback from its customers (and acts on that feedback) will generally have more loyal customers. In addition, the business will focus on what its customers really want, and what they're willing to pay for. All together, these factors can increase the profitability of a business, and therefore its value.

The above four value points are clear and succinctly simple. A core set of business *value-drivers* is (or should be) common to all business organizations.

---

[1] Getting Results - What Makes a Business Valuable?

Published Apr 02, 2007 by PAUL SVENDSEN of Central Oregon Community College

Most Businesses have some attributes that are perceived as **negative** attributes. In the mind of the Buyer, those attributes are seen as *detractors* of value. I refer to them as **value-killers**. And there are many.

Often business owners don't recognize the existence of value-killers in their businesses. And if they are recognized, business owners may not understand the *weight of negative perception* these situations carry.

We will discuss more on *Value-drivers and Value-killers* later but meanwhile you can refer to the "Checklists" section at the back of this guide where I have included an excellent chart that provides a wealth of information on this topic.

Cash Flow: The Ultimate Value-driver

Earlier, we discussed four issues that contribute to business value:
1. Loyal Customers/Employees
2. Systems (in Place)
3. Unique Core Differentiators
4. Customer Focus

Theoretically, these four attributes sound impressive. But they mean little if they do not work together to culminate in the single most crucial issue: **Cash Flow**.

Without adequate cash flow, the prospective Buyer of the business **will not be able to**:

1. Service acquisition debt (I can't emphasize this enough)
2. Finance current business operations
3. Finance future equipment replacement needs
4. Expand to meet customer needs
5. Provide new ownership with adequate management compensation
6. Provide a Buyer with Return on Investment
7. BUY THE BUSINESS!

One of the first questions business Buyers ask is "How much money does the business make?"

They are often stumped when I ask, "When you say 'how much,' do you mean *book* profit, *taxable* profit, or *cash* flow?"

Knowing how much money (cash flow) a business produces is important to potential Buyers. They need this information in order to determine 1) *if they want to buy the business*, 2) *how much they are willing to pay for the business*, and of course 3) *if the cash flow will support the purchase price (financing of the purchase)*.

What is the Difference between Profit and Cash Flow?

It is important to understand that *there is a difference between profits and cash flows.* This guide is not intended to be an all exhaustive treatise on accounting principles. Accordingly, my discussion assumes the reader is either familiar with some basic accounting concepts, or will become familiar. These issues are important to gain a general understanding of because even if the Buyer doesn't understand the difference between profit and cash flow, *his advisors will.* No matter how much the potential Buyer is in love with the business and wants to purchase it, the bank may not finance the acquisition if they don't see adequate cash flow to repay for the loan.

When looking at businesses to acquire, Buyers might ask: *"Are profits reported on a cash basis, an accrual basis, or a generally accepted accounting principles (GAAP) basis?"* Or, *"Are they determined by using a hybrid income tax basis?"*

These are good questions. But regardless of the accounting method used, Buyers and their advisors *will convert the reported profit into cash flow.* Without identifying cash flow, it is extremely difficult for business owners and business Buyers to understand exactly how a business is really performing.

Most businesses keep their accounting records for the purposes of reporting *taxable profit, showing the lowest profit for the lowest possible income tax.* Note: <u>taxable</u> profits are usually much different than <u>financial</u> <u>statement</u> profits. Financial Statement profits are often determined using (GAAP).

No worries though. No matter what accounting basis was used for reporting profits almost any type of profit can easily be converted into cash flow.

How to Convert Profit to Cash Flow

For the purposes of purchasing a business, profit is converted to *cash flow* by converting reported profit into earnings before interest, taxes, depreciation, and amortization expenses (**EBITDA**).

By converting reported profits (either on financial statements or tax returns) into EBITDA, the Buyer, investor and/or banker can gain a better understanding of cash being generated by the business.

> **Insider Tip:** *Banks and Buyers will primarily use tax returns as a starting point for determining EBITDA / cash flow. They figure while business owners may embellish a bit on their financial statements, they will be less likely to do so on their tax returns. Plus any accounting adjustments that happened during the year will be resolved by the time taxes are filed.*

EBITDA is most frequently determined and used in business valuation and business pricing scenarios. This is because EBITDA converts "profits" (which may have been calculated by different companies using different accounting methodologies) into a more common *cash flow*. This makes it much easier to compare results from one operating company to the results of another.

The example on the following page reflects the Fudbucket Company's GAAP Income Statement versus the company's Taxable Profit on the tax return. Tax return profit is smaller than financial statement GAAP profit. But notice at the bottom where the profit under each method, when converted to EBITDA, is exactly the same amount even though the reported profits were different.

Fudbucket Company

	Income Tax Basis	GAAP Basis	Explanation of Differences
Revenues	$ 10,000,000	$ 10,000,000	
Cost of Goods Sold	$ (5,000,000)	$ (5,000,000)	
Gross Profits	$ 5,000,000	$ 5,000,000	
G&A Expenses	$ 1,500,000	$ 1,500,000	
Depreciation Expense	$ 800,000	$ 400,000	Tax Return: elected faster tax depreciation
Amortization Expense	$ 100,000	$ 50,000	Tax Return: elected faster tax amortization
Interest Expense	$ 350,000	$ 250,000	GAAP: elected to capitalize some interest
Total Expenses	$ 2,750,000	$ 2,200,000	
Pre-tax Operating Profit	$ 2,250,000	$ 2,800,000	GAAP Reflects higher profit for shareholder
Less Income Tax	$ (765,000)	$ (952,000)	Tax Return Elections reduce tax costs.
After Tax Profit	$ 1,485,000	$ 1,848,000	Tax Return reflects smaller profit

CONVERTING INTO SIMPLE EBITDA CASH FLOW

	Income Tax Basis	GAAP Basis	Explanation of Differences
Add: Depreciation Expense	$ 800,000	$ 400,000	This is non-cash expense
Add: Amortization Expense	$ 100,000	$ 50,000	This is non-cash expense
Add: Interest Expense	$ 350,000	$ 250,000	Add because Buyer will have different
Add: Income Tax Expense	$ 765,000	$ 952,000	Add because Buyer may have different
Simple EBITDA Cash Flow	$ 3,500,000	$ 3,500,000	

By converting reported profits (either on financial statements or tax returns) into EBITDA, the Buyer, investor and/or banker can gain a better understanding of cash being generated by the business. Again, EBITDA earnings are most frequently used in business valuation and business pricing scenarios. This is because EBITDA converts "profits" (which may have been calculated by different companies using different accounting methodologies) into a more common cash flow. This makes it much easier to compare results from one operating company to the results of another.

> **Insider Tip:** *There are different types of cash flows calculated for various reasons that are too complex for this book's purpose. It is important to note that the cash flow analysis regularly prepared by your CPA is different from EBITDA.*

How to Calculate Your Company's EBITDA

Here is a general method to convert your company's profit into EBITDA:
1. Start with after tax profit
2. Add nonrecurring expenses and owner perks *not necessary to operate the business, etc..*
3. Less nonrecurring income, non-operating income, etc..
4. Equals subtotal of *normalized earnings*
5. Plus Interest Expense
6. Plus Income Tax Expense
7. Plus Depreciation Expense
8. Plus Amortization Expense

Equals ***Earnings before Interest Taxes, Depreciation, Amortization (EBITDA)***

> **Insider Tip:** *EBITDA is a fairly simple method that you can use to measure your company's performance compared to your industry peer group. We'll discuss this in greater detail later.*

Sellers Discretionary Earnings (SDE)

Thus far we have only discussed EBITDA cash flow. EBITDA calculations are most often (but not always) used in valuing mid-market sized companies. Mid-market is usually considered to be businesses with revenues ranging from $2 million to $50 million (depending on which resource you use).

For smaller businesses there is another method for measuring *cash flow*. It is known as *Seller Discretionary Earnings (SDE)*. SDE is most often associated with valuing smaller "main street" type businesses with sales under $2 million, such as restaurants, bars and grills, laundries, auto repair shops, small manufacturers, small machine shops, etc..

You might be wondering why a different cash flow methodology (SDE) is used for smaller businesses rather than the EBITDA methodology used for larger businesses.

Buyers of larger businesses may have different objectives than do the Buyers of smaller businesses. Those acquiring larger companies may place more weight on return on investment (ROI), synergies associated with merging businesses for additional market share, and so on. Also note that different types of Buyers may use slightly different methods of calculating cash flow as well.

> **Insider Tip:** *Private Equity Groups (PEGS) consider the value of cash flows and return on investment (ROI) AFTER salaries have been paid to CEOs and other operating management as they may either keep the current owner on after the sale or will need to bring in outside management. However,* **Buyers of smaller businesses are usually buying a job.** *They will usually self manage and are looking to improve the cash flow benefits to their families. For acquirers of smaller businesses, return on investment isn't the primary reason for buying.*

In small businesses, the only people who might ordinarily see financial and tax records are the business owner, the business owner's accountant, perhaps the bank, and the Internal Revenue Service. Business owners who are not considering selling their business today or in the near future work creatively to minimize income taxes. **They often do this by deducting certain lifestyle expenses through the business.**

While these lifestyle expenditures are *perks* to the business owner, they are not generally critical to the operating of the business; thus it becomes more difficult to show the *true profitability* of the business to a potential Buyer. **This is where SDE comes into play. This adjustment process is often called recasting.**

How to Calculate Your Company's Seller Discretionary Earnings (SDE)

1. Start with after tax profit
2. Add nonrecurring expenses
3. Subtract nonrecurring income, non-operating income, etc., which equals subtotal of *normalized earnings*
4. Add Interest Expense

5. Add Income Tax Expense
6. Add Depreciation Expense
7. Add Amortization Expense
8. Add one owner's salary, wages or compensation
9. Add Employer Payroll Taxes associated with one owner salary
10. Add all other **Owner Fringe Benefits and Perks not critical to the operation of business

Equals *Seller Discretionary Earnings (SDE)*

**All other owner fringe benefits might include things such as: *excess* family salaries/benefits, officer health and life insurances, officer auto, excessive rents paid to owners, motor boat expenses, airplane, vacations, and other personal expenses. You may note the primary difference in calculating the SDE verses EBITDA is how an owner/operator salary is handled.

Before we go on, let's review a bit. The three most common ways of expressing earnings are:

1. *Net Income* (or Net Profit)
2. *EBITDA* (earnings before interest, taxes, depreciation and amortization)
3. *SDE* (Seller Discretionary Earnings)

Net Income is the easiest to identify for a business. This is the bottom-line profit as shown on the tax return or income statement. Though this is the easiest to identify, it is the least useful method of the three. Net Income doesn't *really* tell the story on how profitable the business actually is.

EBITDA is another common way to calculate business earnings. Though it can be calculated for any business, *EBITDA is more useful when businesses are larger in size*. Investors not managing the day-to-day operations will typically use EBITDA because the calculation looks at the earnings without making an adjustment for an owner/operator. They will have already included the expense of a full-time president or manger to run the operation as the ownership may not be directly involved in the day-to-day operations.

SDE (Seller's Discretionary Earnings) is the key to any small business valuation and sale. Buyers of smaller businesses are usually buying a job. They are looking to improve the cash flow benefits to their families. Note that the owner/operators wages are a primary difference in the way SDE is calculated verses EBIDTA. This SDE calculation shows measurable earnings/cash flow of the small business.

As you can see from the discussions above, it becomes imperative to make sure the business Buyer and the business Seller are speaking the same language when it comes to understanding business earnings.

How Much Profit SHOULD My Business Make?

What is Financial Benchmarking?

In the preceding pages, I discussed the differences between profits and cash flows. You have now observed that calculating your company's cash flow will always begin with the amount of profit generated by your business.

It is also important to know how your business profits *measure up* to the profits being earned by your peers in the same industry segment. Consider the following points:

- *If your profits are lower* than the average profit of your peers, the price someone may be willing to pay for your business is likely to be *less than the average price* paid for other businesses like yours

- *If your profits equal* those of your peers, the price someone may be willing to pay for your business could be *similar to the average price* paid for other businesses like yours

- *If your profits are greater* than those of your peers, the price someone may be willing to pay for your business could be higher than the average price paid for other businesses like yours

The dollar amount of profit your business generates is relative to its gross revenue. This is a way of measuring the monetary efficiency of your business operations. By comparing your results (profit/revenue) to the average results (profit/revenue) of your business peer group, you can determine if yours is worse than, equal to, or better than the profits of your peer group. This is called *financial benchmarking* (and sometimes *profit benchmarking*).

Insider Tip: *In business, benchmarking your performance against that of your competitors can propel you to greatness. It can help you establish internal goals, pinpoint market opportunities, exploit competitor weaknesses, and create the kind of esprit de corps to unify and motivate your team.*

Following is a simplistic example of financial benchmarking:

> **EXAMPLE:** *Company ABLE Wiring manufactures electrical wiring harnesses. Sales are $5 million and net operating profit is $500,000. That means that the profit of $500,000 represents 10% of the total $5 million in sales. However, industry research indicates that the median operating profit in this industry (for a company with similar sales volume) is 15%. What might this comparison tell you about company* **ABLE Wiring**?

In the foregoing example, ABLE Wiring was profitable, earning 10 cents on every dollar of sales. But the indication (from peer group data) suggests that the average manufacturer of electrical harnesses makes 15 cents on every dollar in sales. The initial indication is that ABLE Wiring makes only two thirds as much profit as what might be reasonably expected in this industry.

Without a reasonable explanation for the difference in profitability, would a Buyer perceive the value of ABLE Wiring to be on par with the value of other average businesses in the industry? Remember that it is the *Buyer's perception* that counts in the final determination of value.

Suppose you learn that your gross profit margin is 3% lower than your competition's. On $1 million in revenue, that's $30,000 a year more that your competition is making than you are. Is it because their prices are higher or their costs are lower? Does their sales mix include higher margin items that you don't sell, but could sell? Do they have some sweetheart deal for raw materials that you should know about? Do they spend that extra gross profit or does it fall to the bottom line? If they spend it, what do they spend it on? Does it go into their marketing budget? How does their sales-to-marketing ratio compare to yours? If it's higher, what can you learn from their strategy?

If your business does not compare well with its peers in a financial benchmarking analysis, you need to be looking for answers and taking steps to bring your "found issues" back in line.

Always keep in mind that there may be reasonable explanations as to why your numbers don't compare well with your peers. Know what those reasons are and be ready to explain them to Buyers and bankers. Buyers often use benchmarking as a tool to determine sales price they are willing to pay for your business, so explaining anomalies in your benchmarking numbers upfront may have a direct impact on the price a Buyer is willing to pay.

Financial benchmarking is not only used when selling a business but can be very helpful in managing day-to-day business operations.

Some of the more useful financial benchmarks include:

- Gross profit margins
- Operating margins
- Net profit margins
- Sales trends
- Profitability trends
- Inventory turns
- Accounts receivable turns
- Accounts payable turns
- Salary and compensation data
- Revenue per employee
- Average sales per employee
- Cost per employee
- Marketing expense as a percent of revenue
- Revenue to fixed assets ratio

As you can see, benchmarking can tell you where your company falls in comparison to others in your industry. *Analyzing the data will help you find problem areas that you can address — and also show you where your company excels.*

The next step would be to either hire someone to do the benchmarking or tackle the project yourself.

Hiring a Professional

The number one advantage of hiring a professional would of course be the time savings factors and experience. By hiring a professional you would not be taking your valuable time away from operating the business while you gather and analyze the data. Once you've received the report you could concentrate your efforts on making changes where necessary.

The most appropriate person to do this type of job would be a CPA who is <u>also</u> a Certified or Accredited professional in Business Valuation. The firm you hire should have access to an extensive data base of industry data. The CPA/valuator you hire will evaluate your company, identify strengths and problem areas, recommend solutions, and help you measure results. Make sure the engagement includes a conference time to go over the report results. You want to make sure you have a clear understanding of the results and what changes you may want to make going forward.

Do It Yourself Benchmarking

If you have time on your hands and have a good general grasp of financial matters, you may want to do the benchmarking yourself.

Below are some of the best sources of free or low-cost financial data for a wide range of industries.

Tips for do it yourself benchmarking:

- *Use data from <u>similar size companies</u> within your own geographic area, if possible*
- *Use a source that represents a large universe of inputs so that one or two unusual companies don't skew the numbers*
- *Choose the industry group (usually based on <u>NAICS code</u>) that best represents your business*
- *Make sure you read all the notes about the groups you select to include in your analysis. Key information that may cause you to include or exclude a group may be found there*

Ten Free Sources of Industry Financial Data

1. Your specific *industry association* may be the best source for consolidated industry data and financial benchmarks.

2. <u>Internal Revenue Service Corporate Sourcebook</u>: Offers summary balance sheet and income statement numbers for all industries by size of company.

3. <u>Annual reports of public companies in your industry:</u> Order the annual report as well as the 10K and 10Qs. The good stuff often hides in the notes, so read those carefully. Though these companies may be larger than yours, their numbers can offer insights into how they got that way.

4. <u>Bureau of Labor Statistics Labor Productivity and Costs:</u> Shows output per hour and unit labor costs by industry.

5. <u>Bureau of Labor Statistics Labor Pay and Benefits</u>: Provides information on wages, earnings, and benefits by geography, occupation, and industry.

6. <u>Bureau of Labor Statistics Labor Producer Price Index:</u> Offers production cost trend data by industry.

7. <u>US Department of Labor:</u> Reports hours, wages, and earnings reports by industry.

8. <u>US Census Bureau Economic Census:</u> Provides annual and trend data on sales, payroll, and number of employees by industry, product, and geography.

9. <u>US Census Business Expense Survey:</u> Reports sales, inventories, operating expenses, and gross margin by industry.

10. <u>US Census Annual Survey of Manufacturers:</u> Covers employment, plant hours, payroll, fringe benefits, capital expenditures, and cost of materials, inventories, and energy consumption.

Three Inexpensive Sources of Industry Data

1. <u>Dun & Bradstreet</u>: Offers individual company data on sales, employees, net worth, nature of financing, credit worthiness, balance sheet/income statement/ratio data, law suits, public filings, liens, judgments. (Note: some records are more complete than others.)
2. <u>The Risk Management Association:</u> This is the one your bank probably uses to benchmark your performance, so it's well worth the money to know what it says.
3. <u>Morningstar.com:</u> Offers easy access to financial information about public companies.

Example *of Peer Financial Benchmark Data for Manufacturers:*

The following information is an example for the Manufacturing Sector (published in 2010) provided by **First Research Industry Profiles, Inc.** The data represents the mathematical *mean* (average) operating ratios derived from over 260 thousand companies; 169 thousand of those companies had revenues of less than $1 million, and 91 thousand companies had revenues in excess of $1 million.

It is important to understand that there are *more specific industry profile reports* for particular sectors within each general classification. In this guide, I have chosen to use the broad classification for purposes of demonstration.

For a more specific comparison between your business and the sector in which it operates, go to www.microbilt.com/firstresearch where you can purchase at a relativity reasonable price and industry profile more tailored to your particular industry segment.

NOTE: for purposes of this report, the small companies are those with revenues of under $1 million annually.

COMPANY BENCHMARK INFORMATION[2]
NAICS: 31, 32, 33

Data Period	**Last Update 2010**
Small Company Data	**Sales < $1 Million**
Table Data Format	**Mean**

---

[2] Obtained from First Research Industry Profiles, Inc., November 14, 2011 profile for SIC CODES: 2000, 2100, 2200, 2300, 2400, 2500, 2600, 2700, 2800, 2900: NAICS CODES: 31, 32, 33

Example *of Peer Financial Benchmark Data for Manufacturers (Continued):*

	All Companies	**Small Company**
Company Count	260,277	169,141
Income Statement		
Net Sales	100%	100%
Gross Margin	29.5%	33.7%
Officer Compensation	2.1%	3.9%
Advertising & Sales	0.7%	0.8%
Other Operating Expenses	23.2%	25.3%
Operating Expenses	25.9%	30.0%
Operating Income	3.6%	3.7%
Net Income	1.6%	1.7%
Balance Sheet		
Cash	9.0%	9.2%
Accounts Receivable	21.6%	22.1%
Inventory	19.6%	20.7%
Total Current Assets	57.6%	59.7%

Example *of Peer Financial Benchmark Data for Manufacturers (Continued):*

	All Companies	**Small Company**
Property, Plant & Equipment	24.5%	22.8%
Other Non-Current Assets	18.0%	17.5%
Total Assets	100.0%	100.0%
Accounts Payable	12.0%	12.2%
Total Current Liabilities	27.8%	29.6%
Total Long Term Liabilities	26.2%	30.8%
Net Worth	46.0%	39.5%

Financial Ratios

If you are reading a computerized copy of the book, click on any ratio for comprehensive definitions.

	All Companies	**Small Company**
Quick Ratio	1.18	1.15
Current Ratio	2.07	2.011
Current Liabilities to Net Worth	60.3%	75.0%
Current Liabilities to Inventory	x1.41	x1.43
Total Debt to Net Worth	x1.17	x1.53

Example *of Peer Financial Benchmark Data for Manufacturers (Continued):*

	All Companies	Small Company
Fixed Assets to Net Worth	x0.53	x0.58
Days Accounts Receivable	51	48
Inventory Turnover	x5.55	x5.40
Total Assets to Sales	68.2%	62.6%
Working Capital to Sales	20.3%	18.8%
Accounts Payable to Sales	7.7%	7.2%
Pre-Tax Return on Sales	2.7%	2.8%
Pre-Tax Return on Assets	3.9%	4.5%
Pre-Tax Return on Net Worth	8.5%	11.3%
Interest Coverage	x2.72	x2.93
EBITDA to Sales	6.7%	7.2%
Capital Expenditures to Sales	5.1%	5.2%

Financial industry data above provided by MicroBilt Corporation – Integra Financial Benchmarking Data for detailed Business Valuation and analysis data from over 900 industries (SIC & NAICS) and 13 sales size ranges. 2010 data and historical data from 1998-2009 available by subscription or purchase single report at www.microbilt.com/firstresearch.

Identifying the Value-Killers and Value-Builders

As an experienced Certified Public Accountant, Certified Valuation Analyst, Accredited Business Valuator, Certified Business Intermediary (Business Broker) and Master Analyst in Financial Forensics, I have been involved in the sale of numerous businesses and in turn have dealt with hundreds of Buyers' *due diligence procedures* on many different levels.

This is a good time to bring up due diligence. **Due diligence** is what the Buyer does when exploring the possible purchase of a company. Usually due diligence is performed in two parts 1) Pre-Letter of Intent (LOI) or Contingent Purchase Offer (CPO) due diligence and 2) Post-LOI due diligence.

In Pre-LOI due diligence, Buyers ask general questions: they may ask for management's projections for the future, growth estimates, tax returns, depreciation schedules, financial statements, etc.. These items are generally enough information to allow the Buyer to make a CPO or a LOI, subject to Post-LOI due diligence procedures.

Once the Buyer and Seller agree to the general terms of the LOI or contingent purchase offer, the Buyer will commence **Post-LOI due diligence.** *If the Buyer and Seller can't come to an agreement with respect to <u>general terms and conditions</u>, there will not be a reason that the Seller would want to reveal more in-depth confidential operating information about his business to a potential Buyer.*

In Post-LOI due diligence, the Buyer is looking for as much in-depth information about the business as possible: accounting records verification, personnel records, legal activity/lawsuits, environmental issues, safety issues, customer issues, vendor issues, technology issues, requirements for future capital expenditures, etc..

The Post-LOI due diligence is where a Buyer looks for all the warts and skeletons; things that make the business less desirable.

If you've never been through due diligence (as a Seller), it can best be described as *"having your tonsils examined by a proctologist!"* In other words it's not FUN and a lot of work. But you have to wear the Buyers' shoes for a minute. Wouldn't you like to know exactly what you were buying?

By following the suggestions in this guide, you and your business should better be able to survive (and thrive) during the due diligence process.

> **Insider Tip:** *Often a Buyer wants to see EVERYTHING under God's green earth before general purchase terms are agreed on. Managing the flow of confidential information is one of the many jobs a professional Certified Business Intermediary handles. It is important to keep the Buyer's requests realistic. Neither party wants to waste time and money in the investigation of a business purchase that won't fundamentally work.*

In my role as a **Certified Public Accountant**, potential business Buyers have often engaged my services to assist in the performance due diligence on a Seller's business. I look for any red flags and facts about a prospective acquisition target that may be considered unfavorable to a Buyer. The perceived negative issues say much about the risks associated with the business. The higher the risk the lower the perceived value of the business being considered. In some cases the perceived risks associated with the business are such that the Seller's business was not sellable under the existing circumstances.

In my capacity as a **Certified Valuation Analyst**, I am often asked for my professional opinion with regard to business values for sale, buy-sell agreements, divorce, gifting, estate settlement, and recapitalization. It is my job to look for both the beautiful and ugly attributes of a business. The beautiful attributes (*value-drivers*) tend to reduce risk, or increase value. And the ugly attributes (*value-killers*) increase risk and diminish perceptions of value. These considerations are imperative in my final *Opinion of Value*. It is important to note that my opinion is based in part on my combined perceptions of the positive points and negative points associated with the business being valued.

As a **Certified Business Intermediary (Business Broker)**, my job is to analyze and confidentially market and sell a client's business. If we determine that a business is not marketable or sellable in its current condition, we decline the sales engagement.

When at all possible, we work with the Seller to help target the issues that a Buyer might perceive as negative. Reducing the negative issues can add value to a business, which is often the owner's life work.

Sometimes the issues that need dealt with are small in nature and can be completed in short order. But more often, when an owner has not considered how the business will appear to a potential Buyer, it takes more time to get the business in shape for a sale.

Owners are in business to make money. They are busy dealing with the day to day challenges that are part of running a business. However, if you put on a Buyer's hat every once in awhile, you will be able to make changes here and there as you go along. ***By making small changes as you operate your business, you will be much more prepared if you <u>need</u> to sell in an unexpected circumstance.***

Below is a list of the most common *"value-killers"* that can be found in many businesses.

Business Value-killers

- Heavy reliance on the owner
- Lack of profitability/cash flow
- Under-reported income
- Overstated expenses (personal expenses intermingled with business expenses)
- Incorrectly reported inventory
- Incorrect work-in-progress inventory
- Overstated inventory (*inaccurate inventory count/pricing*)
- Downward trend in sales and profits
- Co-mingled business and personal assets
- Operating assets vs. non operating assets
- Outdated products and services
- Outdated information and operating technologies
- Outdated bookkeeping/accounting systems
- Labor union contracts (*union problems*)
- High employee turnover
- Environmental issues
- Safety issues
- Regulatory issues
- Customer concentration issues

- Industry concentration issues
- Competitive pressures
- Appearances

Do you recognize any of these issues in your business? Some of the foregoing circumstances will, all by themselves, make a business worth significantly less or even unsellable. Combine several of these examples and you tend to create killer situations which can really hurt your wallet.

In the following segments I will address each of these adverse circumstances and provide you with suggestions for eliminating business value-killers. And as with everything in this guide, seek qualified and experienced professionals to help guide you in your particular situation.

Heavy Reliance on the Owner

One of the most common *value-killers* in any business is a *company's heavy reliance on the services of the owner to maintain and keep the operation running*. The individual whose personal services account for the majority of business transactions doesn't own a business. Rather, that individual owns a job.

The business owner who micro-manages almost every detail of the business is not building value in the company. To the contrary, the owner is diminishing the value of the business. An example:

The Man Who Did it All

In a previous book, I told the story about a very prosperous graphic designer who operated three locations. He would spend time in all three offices each and every week. He did the job price quoting, client billing, paid the bills, did the accounting, approved concepts, maintained all client contact, tried to review each and every job before it went out the door, and he still found time to bill 20 to 30 creative hours per week!

The poor guy worked seven days a week and at least part of most holidays. *He died of a heart attack in his 50s*.

The widow said that their plan was for him to work until he was sixty, sell the business, and have plenty of money to retire with.

The deceased business owner's son and wife called me in to talk about selling the business. What I learned was disheartening. Neither the wife nor the son had any idea about the business operations. They said that each location had an office manager, but the managers knew nothing about the real business workings. The managers were merely traffic managers—setting up production schedules and assigning personnel. The managers had very little contact with clients and knew nothing about price quotes, etc..

Without the owner, the company was floundering. The company ultimately sold for about 30% of the amount it could have sold for under the proper circumstances. This devastated the finances and threw retirement plans out the window.

Note: the issue wasn't that the family didn't know how to run the business. The problem was that there was not anyone on the staff who knew how to successfully operate the business.

Keys to Success

Recently we sold a very successful company for a premium price. One of the largest factors that added value to the business was the *ownership's lack of involvement in the day-to-day business operations.*

The company was owned by a husband and wife. The couple decided in their mid-40s that they wanted to sell the company and retire when they were in their early 50s. They did more than just talk about it. Here are some of the steps they took:

- Administrative—Trained a primary and a backup bookkeeper/office manager for front office operations. The wife continued part-time in Human Resources until that function was farmed out to an outside agency.

- Sales—The husband hired and trained a business development manager who was paid a base salary, commission, and bonuses on achieving certain volumes of business. The business development manager was also trained to quote profitable jobs.

- Engineering—The husband worked with the existing engineers to develop documentation of process and systems. Then an assistant engineering manager was trained and developed.

- Operations—The husband developed an operations manual and then trained two long-time employees in company philosophies, internal workings, processes, scheduling and delivery systems. The two employees traded off every other week as acting plant manager and acting traffic manager. That way, each could perform both jobs.

- Computer operations—The husband hired an experienced data and technology person. Together they created systems and reports to help better manage the business. Eventually an assistant technology manager was hired to provide back-up to the primary technology manager.

- Plant—The husband, after getting others trained, was able to spend time to develop better work flow logistics and an improved materials handling process. He then trained someone else to perform these duties.

When I first met this couple to discuss the sale of their business, they answered my first question perfectly.

"What do you do at the company?" I asked.

"We just get in the way...then we decide to take another vacation. They don't really need us there anymore," was their answer.

Their answer was purely golden and one I rarely hear. We sold their company for a very high multiple of the company's EBITDA (earnings before interest expense, taxes, depreciation and amortization). And oh, by the way, this was an all-cash deal!

Lack of Profitability and Cash Flow

A conversation I have almost daily. My administrative assistant tells me that there is a prospective business Seller on the phone. I take the call and chat with the business owner for a bit. I ask the potential Seller why he wants to sell the business. All too often the answer is the same: *"We're just not making good money anymore!"*

The most common culprit for making a business undesirable and unsellable is the lack of profitability and cash flow. Sellers need to understand the *majority of business Buyers are not interested in buying a loss.* Buyers don't want your headaches and problems. They don't want to deplete their own capital to repair the cash flow ills of your business. While there may occasionally be situations where business Buyers want only the Seller's customer list, territory, or intangible properties, these cases are the exception and not the rule.

Sometimes Sellers will say to me, *"Well, if the new owner would do this, and this, or that—the business would be worth their while."*

The reality is this: no Buyer is going to pay you, the Seller, for what they will invest in time and money to bring the business up to par. If the Seller wants to get a higher sales price, then it is incumbent upon the *Seller* to *"do this, and this, and/or that."*

There may be many reasons why a business is not profitable on paper. Some successful businesses "look" like they lose money, when in reality they are more successful than they appear. These situations are usually caused by "creative" accounting strategies that have been employed to reduce income taxes. This situation is the easiest one to remedy. I'll discuss this in greater detail in following chapters. Many other causes for lack of profitability and a discussion of possible solutions will also be addressed.

Before going further, I think it very important to say that it is not always impossible to sell a business that is *losing money*. There is a class of Buyer known as *"bottom feeders"* (many refer to themselves as *turnaround specialists*). These Buyers are always on the lookout for *loss or underperforming businesses* that **can be purchased for very little**. If the *specialist* thinks there is any possibility of turning the business around, or even if money can be made in a total liquidation, then there is a chance that the business can be sold...*at a very deep discount*. So, if you are willing to sell your business at a discount, I can save you some time. Stop reading here! You don't need to read the remainder of this guide.

Under-Reported Income

Occasionally I receive calls from business owners who tell me their businesses are extremely profitable and should easily sell. But when reviewing the business tax returns, I find anything but a profitable business. When I discuss the issue with the owners, many smile and tell me that they have not reported all the income on the

34

books. That is when I and most other reputable Business Brokers walk away from the business.

Gambling with the Tax Collector

Apparently, some folks are not afraid of the Internal Revenue Service and other taxing authorities. It is a well-known fact that the Internal Revenue Service is one of the most powerful collection agencies in the world. Business owners who under-report income are taking substantial risks of audit, tax assessments, penalties, interest assessments, and in some cases, even jail!

My advice to business Buyers who are considering purchasing a business from an owner who has cheated on his taxes is always the same: *"If the Seller has no fear of, and will cheat one of the most powerful collection agencies in the world, he will certainly not be afraid to cheat you!"*

Bad Perception

A Seller should never tell a prospective Buyer *"not all the business income has been reported."* The Seller usually doesn't actually put it in those words. It might be more like the wink of an eye and a smile. When a Seller makes these types of statements, it puts the **perception** into the Buyer's head that maybe other aspects of the Seller's accounting have been inaccurate. This increases perceived risk and reduces perceived value in the business.

In addition, the Buyer may perceive that he is dealing with a Seller who may not live up to any agreements that they may make in a deal; this can lead to costly litigation—which nobody wants to endure. Another negative: the Buyer may get the perception that the Seller will be a "difficult character" in future dealings. These negative perceptions will either drive the Buyer's perception of value down, or will drive the Buyer away from the deal completely.

Many business owners don't understand that under-reporting *income costs them much more than the tax savings...even if the IRS never catches up with them!* Next I'll explain how under-reporting income can cost a business owner up to *ten times the amount they think they have "saved in taxes."*

Unreported Income Cheats the Business Owner

> **EXAMPLE:** Assume Slippery Joe decides to skim (not report) $40,000 of income from his business. He does so by pocketing $40,000 income and not reporting it on his tax return. Slippery Joe knows that his total tax rate is about 40% so he figures that he has saved $16,000 in taxes (Multiply $40,000 by 40%).
>
> Slippery Joe decided he would like to move somewhere warmer and needs to sell his business. The business intermediary (broker) tells Slippery Joe that this type of business may sell for approximately 4 times EBITDA (earnings before interest, taxes, depreciation and amortization expense). But Joe's tax return now reflects a profit that is $40,000 short…because Joe decided to cheat Uncle Sam out of $16,000 in taxes. $40,000 in profit using a multiplier of 4 indicates $160,000 in value; i.e. a higher sales price. Joe is going to have a tough time trying to get that extra $160,000 from a Buyer (he won't get it). But, he did save $16,000 in taxes (assuming he is never audited). Just how smart is Slippery Joe?

Case History

Before we sold our CPA practice years ago, we had a client who produced very specific parts for airplanes. I'll call the client Devious Dick. Unbeknown to us, Dick would fly certain parts to customers all across the country and pocket the cash sales. He made the mistake of letting his office manager in on his devious dealings.

Dick called me one day and asked me to perform a business valuation. He was thinking about moving to a warmer climate and was considering selling the business. I valued the business at $1,000,000 (not knowing about the unreported income). Keep in mind that if he had reported all income, this valuation would have been much higher.

Dick called me about a week after we presented the business valuation. He informed me that his office manager and her boyfriend were interested in buying his business. The perspective buyers offered Dick $600,000 "or else." I asked Dick what "or else" meant. Dick explained that the office manager would leave employment with the company unless Dick sold the business for $600,000. Dick wasn't very happy, but ultimately decided that he could not sacrifice the business for a mere $600,000. He smiled and said he thought he'd have to endure the "or else" part of the offer. We both laughed.

About four months after the office manager left Dick's employment, Dick found out the other part of the "or else" offer. He was visited by an IRS auditor. Ultimately, the U.S. Treasury's Criminal Investigative division began investigating Dick. They soon uncovered where he had been personally skimming an average of $250,000 per year in the cash sale of parts. He had been doing this for over 4 years! (Dick lived in an average home, drove a rusty old pickup and could always be seen wearing raggedy blue jeans and a faded work shirt. He sure didn't look extravagant!)

What we have learned:

1. Devious Dick cheated himself out of an additional potential sale value of about $750,000 to $1,000,000 ($250,000 times a multiplier of from 3 to 4).
2. The "trusted employee" and her boyfriend were ready to take advantage of a discounted business at only $600,000 when they knew its true worth was much greater.
3. Devious Dick received IRS deficiency notices for back taxes, penalties and interest totaling $2.5 million.
4. Dick received free room and boarding at a federal prison for three years; he had nothing upon leaving prison.

My advice about unreported business income is the same to all business owners: don't be a "Dick." Report all business income. Use only legal tax reduction methods. Any business owner who is thinking about selling their business should review their income reporting habits and history. In some cases it's best to go back and amend tax returns and pay the piper. You should get a higher sale price when you eventually sell your business. The increased sales price will more than cover what you might have saved in taxes *and* you will sleep better at night.

Overstated Expenses

The business owner who overstates business expenses is also taking substantial risks of audit, tax assessments, penalties and interest assessments. Overloading expenses and the cost of sales has almost become a science to some business owners. In addition to increased risk of tax audit, overstated expenses might send potential Buyers running for cover.

Detection May be Easy

Overstating business expenses is the act of reporting more expenses than were required to operate a business in a normal manner (by deducting such things as home and personal expenses on the business books). Overstated operating expenses may be detected during a Buyer's due diligence procedures.

Business Buyers often perform a financial *benchmarking analysis* on a Seller's business. Various industry data sources are available that provide operating ratios and analysis for almost every type of industry. CPAs, bankers, investors and other financial analysts (including the IRS) rely upon published industry data to make comparisons with your business.

Let's say that the average percentage of sales for cost of goods sold (in your industry for a business your size) is 38%. But your company's cost of goods sold is 48%. It's easy to see that your cost to produce revenue is 10% higher than what your average peer experiences. This will cause questions that a Seller/owner needs to be ready with a realistic answer.

In this scenario a Buyer will see that there is something obviously different about your business operations compared to your peers:

1. Maybe your business records classify cost of sales differently than others in your peer group, or
2. Maybe there are inefficiencies in your operation which cause Cost of Goods to be higher than experienced by your peers (this is not a good thing), or
3. Maybe your cost of sales includes *the cost of personal items, home improvements, etc.*

As discussed earlier, some business owners think that by burying personal expenses in with business expenses, they are saving tax dollars. Unfortunately, this type of thinking may actually be costing the business owner several times what has been saved in income taxes.

If personal expenses have not been deducted and the cost of sales percentage is *still higher than that of a statistical peer group*; other warning signs are being signaled to a potential Buyer. This situation is indicative of additional risks associated with your business, causing the prospective Buyer to devalue your business.

Know When to Add Back…and When to Amend

In my many years of experience valuing and selling businesses, I have been told about all manner of personal types of expenses that business owners have buried in their expense accounts. Some of the personal expenses are relatively small to moderate; most business brokers and bankers don't mind adding small amounts back to the profit of the business for purpose of calculating SDE or EBITDA. **Note:** *the term "adding back" is referring to increasing reported profit by the dollar amount of items that were deducted on the tax return/financial statements that the business owner was not entitled to deduct.*

> **Insider Tip**: *If you have small or moderate personal expenses "buried" in your financial statements, it is much better to disclose upfront versus letting the Buyer or his advisors find them. The Buyer will then worry about what else you haven't told him!*

When I encounter glaringly large personal add-backs, I always advise that the business owner should file amended income tax returns and pay the income taxes due. We advise this course of action because:

1. If the business owner voluntarily files amended tax returns, they reduce the risk of incurring severe civil and criminal penalties.
2. If the business owner amends the tax returns, prospective Buyers may perceive that the business Seller is honest and willing to make right any "mistakes." This may tend to *reduce risk and increase perceived business value.*
3. The amended returns which reflect higher profits and higher taxes help substantiate a higher valuation, and thus a higher price for the business.
4. Each dollar paid in higher taxes may be worth from $2.50 to $5.00 in a higher sale price.

Some examples of egregious expenses (personal expenses Sellers bury in business expense accounts) that I have seen include:

- Wedding expenses (tens of thousands of dollars) buried in advertising expense and/or cost of goods sold
- Personal home remodeling expenses buried in cost of goods sold

39

- Ski-mobiles and snowmobiles bought and expensed as repairs and maintenance
- Breast implants being expensed as advertising and promotion
- Extravagant trips to exotic places written off as meeting expenses
- Cost of horses and horse boarding written off as advertising
- Repairs made to personal boats and airplanes deducted as business operating expenses
- And more…

As anyone can see, expenses like the above examples would be deemed by the IRS or Buyers Advisors as excessive and egregious. (This could mean additional tax, interest and penalties).

If a business owner is thinking about selling the business and has the foregoing issues he/she might consider the following:

- Because Buyers, Investors and Bankers consider (at minimum) the most recent three years' tax returns, amend the tax returns for the most recent three years so that *at least* those returns are correct and accurate.

- If a business owner is not willing to amend the tax returns, then I advise them to stop writing off the large non-business expenses for two or three years before trying to sell the business.

Over-reporting business expenses is part of the *lack of profit and lack of cash flow scenarios*. Positive (and sizable) cash flow is extremely important in the valuation and sale of your business.

I urge anyone who might be thinking about the sale of their company within two or three years to examine their treatment of personal expenses before showing any potential Buyer any type of financial statement or tax return. First impressions can be lasting impressions. *Clean tax returns and accounting records are ways of putting your best foot forward while increasing the value of your business*.

Incorrectly Reported Inventory

Business inventory is an asset. Accounting for the costs associated in inventory has a bearing on 1) the value of business assets and 2) the amount of profit or loss reflected on the financial statements. An accurate inventory is necessary to clearly show income when the production, purchase, or sale of merchandise is an income-producing factor in your business

To properly calculate "taxable" income, an owner would need to value inventory at the beginning and ending of each tax year. To determine the value, you will need a consistent method for identifying the items in your inventory and a method for valuing these items.

> **Insider Tip:** *The rules for valuing inventory are not the same for all kinds of businesses. The method used must conform to generally accepted accounting principles for similar businesses and must clearly reflect income. Inventory practices must be consistent from year to year.*

A very common accounting (and tax) dilemma can be found in both small and large businesses. This dilemma involves accounting for the *true cost of inventory*.

A higher inventory level at year-end means lower cost of sales and higher profit: thus higher income taxes.

A lower inventory value at year end means a higher cost of sales, equaling lower profits and lower income taxes.

As you can see from above it is crucial to start with and report a true Inventory amount.

Incorrect Work in Progress Inventory

In some smaller construction and manufacturing environments, I occasionally see where business owners fail to account for the value of *work in progress* at year end. Usually it is not taken into account on financial documents because the business owner does not want to pay income tax on profits that haven't yet been realized as cash.

My question to the construction and business owner is always this: "If you would have sold your business as of the year just ended, would you have just given the work in progress away....for zero dollars?"

Not surprisingly, most owners say "No."

Later, we will look at a couple of scenarios involving the work in progress issue. But first we need to have a general understanding of how Work in Progress and Unbilled Work in Progress are calculated.

Work in Progress is comprised of three elements:

- **Direct Materials**–Materials that become an integral part of the finished product are consumed in the progress and are identified with specific units or progresses.
- **Direct Labor**–Labor which can be associated with particular units. Labor includes basic compensation, overtime pay, vacation and holiday pay, sick leave pay, and payroll taxes.
- **Indirect Costs**–Costs necessary for production other than direct production costs. Indirect costs include variable and fixed overhead.

When looking to sell a construction company or other type of company where work in progress inventory is an issue, it is extremely important to consider the *cost invested* in work in progress. Failure to do so can reduce the sales price by the value of the work in progress as well as a reduction in goodwill calculations *(reduced inventory/work in progress reduces profit which in turn can reduce goodwill value)*.

Understanding Unbilled Work in Progress

Unbilled Work in Progress is comprised of four components:

- **Direct Materials**
- **Direct Labor**
- **Indirect Costs**
- **Profit on percentage of completion** – This is the amount of profit that would be allocated to the work in progress IF it would have been billed (invoiced) to the customer as of the accounting cut-off date.

Note: *percentage of completion* is not used by all production businesses, nor does it need to be. However, in a job shop where specific projects are done on a per-item basis rather than by process (100,000 Widgets) a percentage of completion should be considered, at least for valuation purposes.

The complexities of cost accounting and capitalizing inventory costs are well beyond the scope of this guide. However, business owners need to be aware that improper accounting of inventory can be hazardous to the Seller's financial health when selling the business.

Again, this guide is not intended to be a treatise on accounting, cost accounting or tax accounting. But when calculating the "true profit" of the production type business, one should, at a minimum, account for the cost invested in work in progress.

Demonstrating the Differences in Inventory Valuations

Following is a comparison between reporting a correct inventory and reporting *short-valued* inventories:

Beginning of Year Inventory	$200,000
Purchases Added During Year	+900,000
Total Available for Sale	$1,100,000*
Less *(assumed correct)* end inventory	250,000
Cost of Sales	$850,000

Let's assume that Sales for the year amounted to $1,100,000. The **correct cost of sales** equals $850,000. This means that the Gross Profit on Sales is $250,000 calculated as follows:

Sales for the Year	$ 1,100,000
Less Cost of Sales	850,000
Gross Profit	$ 250,000

Now let's assume that the business *owner wants to significantly reduce* income taxes paid. The owner decides to **report ending inventory of only $150,000.** Let's take a look:

Total Available for Sale $1,100,000* (from above example)

Less *(understated)* end inventory   150,000

Cost of Sales $950,000

With sales of $1,100,000, less the recalculated *(based on a wrong inventory valuation)* cost of sales amounting to $950,000, the newly-calculated Gross Profit on Sales is calculated as follows:

Sales for the year $1,100,000

Less Cost of Sales   - 950,000

Gross Profit Margin $ 150,000

Understating the ending inventory by $100,000 caused the gross profit to shrink by $100,000. This means that bottom line profit (and thus EBITDA) has shrunk by $100,000. This might mean a tax savings of $40,000 if the business is in the 40% income tax bracket.

But, did the company really save $40,000? Remember the examples given in the discussion of unreported income and overstated expenses?

If this business were to sell for a 2.5 multiple to 5.0 multiple of its EBITDA, then cutting the inventory short by $100,000 will reduce indicated business value by anywhere from $250,000 to $500,000. That is a large loss of value and means less in your pocket when you sell.

How to Avoid the Double-Whammy

The immediately preceding example could produce an even worse dilemma. Some business transaction reporting services (they keep track of business sales prices as compared to EBITDA, revenues, and other benchmarks) do not include the value of inventory in their price multiples. In short...their indicated values include only the value of furniture, fixtures, equipment and goodwill. One example of this is the Bizcomps[3] transaction database. The pricing multiples provided exclude the value of inventories.

Assuming the examples I used in this chapter, an indicated price multiple of 2.5 applied to underreported income of $100,000 produces a product of $250,000. But that needs to be adjusted by adding the value of inventory. Because the owner shorted the inventory by $100,000 (to save $40,000 in taxes), the indication of underreported value becomes $350,000! This is the $250K plus the $100K.

I am reminded of something my father told me when I was young, and I am sure you have heard it too: "There's no such thing as a free lunch." When business owners try to outfox the taxing agencies, they sometimes outfox themselves.

Over Stated Inventory

Business Buyers are also cautious of *overvalued inventories.* A business Buyer does not want to invest capital in inventory that will not turn over on a timely basis. The Business Buyer is not interested in the time and expense that it will cost to eliminate *dead* inventories. In fact, many Buyers will discount their offer price if they believe there is significant dead inventory that must be liquidated (and in some cases—hauled to the landfill).

Some business owners are pack rats. They save and account for every possible piece of obsolete inventory in their possession. Or, they over-value inventory for other reasons.

This may be especially true if the business is underperforming. The owner may need to show the bankers good profit margins and a strong balance sheet. Keep in mind that an inflated inventory will reflect profits that are higher than actual. Also, the overstated inventory makes the balance sheet (and working capital) appear to be healthier than it actually is.

Financial Benchmarking for Inventory Issues

Financial benchmarking (as discussed earlier) is an excellent tool to help identify ratios in your business that may indicate unusual inventory levels. Be assured that a

---

[3] www.bizcomps.com

savvy Buyer will compare your company's inventory *turnover ratio* with an industry benchmark.

The turnover ratio is simply Cost of Goods Sold *divided* by the average inventory (COGS/Average Inventory).

This *turnover ratio* should be compared against your industry averages. A low turnover implies poor sales and, therefore excess inventory. A high ratio implies either strong sales or ineffective buying. High inventory levels are unhealthy because they represent an investment bearing a rate of return of zero. It also opens the company up to trouble should prices begin to fall.

Things to remember about Inventory Turnover:

- A low turnover is usually a bad sign because products tend to deteriorate as they sit in a warehouse.

- Companies selling perishable items should have very high turnover.

- For more accurate inventory turnover figures, the average inventory figure— (beginning inventory + ending inventory) divided by 2 are used when computing inventory turnover. Average inventory accounts for any seasonality effects on the ratio.

Suggestions for Improvement

If your company has excess inventory, here is an idea that can help you obtain a greater yield from the sale of your company.

- Identify excess assets that can be converted into cash before a sale transaction, without adversely impacting the business. For example, assuming a company has accumulated $550,000 of inventory but only requires a $350,000 inventory level, the Seller might be able to generate an additional $100,000 to $200,000 by converting the excess inventory to cash. By reducing excess inventory in advance, it provides time to verify that the reduction of these assets will not have a negative impact on earnings. This is important to do prior to a business sale transaction since a Buyer will likely value the company primarily based on earnings and will not be interested in paying for excess inventory.

What I'd like you to take away from the preceding discussion is that inventory valuation plays a huge role in determining business profits and business values. It might pay for you to review with your CPA the methodology you use for inventory valuation. Please be assured that any Buyer of your company will ask many questions about the inventory method you use.

Downward Trend in Sales and Profits[4]

Prospective business Buyers, investors and lenders are cautious, and always on the lookout for declines in sales and profits. Downward trends are ill perceived. Accordingly, the *value of a company usually declines as revenues weaken*. Conversely, as *revenue and profit increases, so does the business value*.

To identify strengths or weaknesses in your revenue stream, prospective Buyers will perform a *trend analysis* on your revenues and profits. So I suggest that potential business Sellers preemptively perform the trend analysis long before a prospective Buyer is ever introduced. A Seller, equipped with positive results, can reduce risks *perceived* by a Buyer. On the other hand, if the Seller understands the nature of a downward trend, steps might be taken to improve trends before placing the company on the market.

What is Trend Analysis?[5]

Trend analysis is the procedure to calculate the percentage of change for one or more accounts on a company's financial statement over a period of two years or more.

Percentage of Change

Percentage of Change calculations can be applied to income accounts, expense accounts and even balance sheet accounts. In the following example, we are using "Sales" which is an income account. To calculate the percentage of change between two periods:

---

[4] http://www.cliffsnotes.com/study_guide/Trend-Analysis.topicArticleId-21248,articleId-21211.html

[5] CliffsNotes.com. *Trend Analysis*. 22 Nov 2011
    <http://www.cliffsnotes.com/study_guide/topicArticleId-21248,articleId-21211.html>.

1. Select a financial statement account to analyze. Calculate the amount of the increase or (decrease) for the period by *subtracting the earlier year account balance from the later year account balance. If the difference is negative, the change is a decrease; if the difference is positive, it is an increase.*

2. Divide the change by the earlier year's account balance. The result is the percentage change.

Calculation of Change Example:

	Last Year	One Year Earlier	Increase/(Decrease)	Percent Change
Sales	129,000	103,000	26,000	25.2%

The example presented above compares only two years of sales activity. It is intended to show you the mechanics of calculating a percent of change. In actual scenarios, sales analysis is performed on five or more years.

Let's assume the following seven year sales trend information:

Year>	Year 1	Year 2	Year 3	Year 4	Year 5	Year 6	Year 7
Sales>	$ 1,900,000	$ 1,862,000	$ 1,694,420	$ 1,829,974	$ 1,958,072	$ 2,075,556	$ 2,096,312
Change	Base Year	-2.00%	-9.00%	8.00%	7.00%	6.00%	1.00%

The chart indicates moderately positive recent trend, though over seven years, the trend is little more than flat. It would be important to learn the reason for the down years, and investigate anticipated growth or decline in future years.

TREND LINE

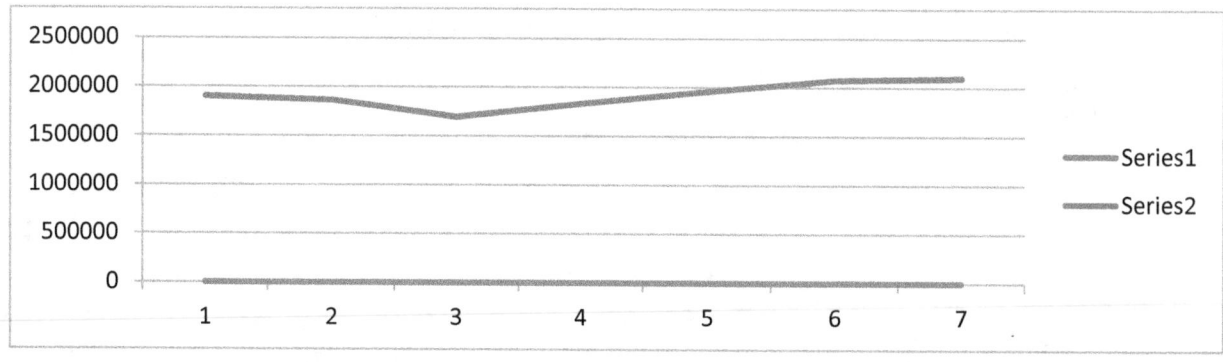

Co-Mingled Business and Personal Assets

From time to time I find business Sellers who, somewhere along the line, decided to put everything (or at least most of what) they own (personal assets) under one corporate roof. Undoubtedly, these folks have been told that this tactic is a wonderful tax saving strategy. This is not so!

They put their autos, homes, vacation condos, rental properties, motor coaches, airplanes, motorcycles, classic autos, cigarette boats, sailboats, antique gun collections and every other *non-business asset* into their *business corporation*. Then they deduct expenses associated with the non-business assets to reduce actual business profits.

The Fly in the Ointment

Sooner or later the business owner is going to exit the business. Unfortunately, the financial statements and tax returns do not clearly reflect what the business actually made. Although the Seller can easily identify and remove the personal assets from the sale, the expense accounts have been cluttered with non-business expenses. Often there is no practical way to truly separate business from non-business items/expenses. And the business owner may not want to separate the expenses for fear of leaving a paper trail for the IRS.

A key consideration in determining the value of any business is the ***quality of the financial reporting*** for business operations. If straightforward and clean accountings of the business operations have not been the norm, *then Buyers perceive risk.* Why? The answer has to do with the reliability of the reported earnings. As the perception of the reliability of reported earnings diminishes, the perceived value of the business also diminishes.

Nobody Wants to Buy a Grab Bag

It has been my experience that the majority of Buyers want to only purchase the business operations and assets directly related to business operations. Some Buyers may not even want to acquire the business operation's associated real estate. Buyers want to purchase only what are 100% money making assets and they need to be able to project returns on the capital invested in specific operations.

As we discussed before when Buyers perform due diligence on a target business, they most often want to review the business balance sheets and the income statements. One of the goals is to develop key financial and operating ratios. These ratios will then be *benchmarked* against peers within the industry.

If a company's ratios are superior to industry averages, this can add to the perceived business value. If a company's ratios are inferior to industry averages, then the perceived business value will diminish.

How can business Buyers develop operating and financial ratios for a business where the balance sheets and income statements are *cluttered with non-operating/personal items?*

Buyers will not expend resources to straighten out the poor accounting practices employed by the Seller. If the financial statements of a Seller's business resemble a grab bag containing a little of this and a little of that the prospective Buyer will be out the door very quickly.

Operating Assets vs. Non Operating Assets

It is important that you have an understanding of the difference between operating and non-operating assets that your company owns. When it is time to sell your business, most Buyers will want only the operating assets.

Operating assets are those assets that *are* directly or indirectly involved in producing your company's main source of revenue.

Non-operating assets are those *not* directly or indirectly involved in the production of your company's main source of revenue.

Make sure that these assets are not all grouped together as only one class of fixed asset on your balance sheet. This will become crucial when it is time for a Buyer to perform due diligence on your company.

Let's assume your company manufactures injection molded plastic consumer products.

Operating Asset	Non-Operating Asset
Injection presses	Investment in adjacent rental property
CNC machines used for making molds	Airplane occasionally used on sales calls
Compound mixing machine	Accounts receivable from related party
Materials handling equipment	Investment in bank stock
Heat treatment ovens	Investment in undeveloped real estate

The assets in the above table demonstrate how assets should be grouped separately under fixed assets. You may need to discuss the presentation of operating assets and non-operating assets with your CPA.

Outdated Products and Services

Our firm has represented many Sellers of enterprises. No matter what product each company manufactured, all of the companies have had one thing in common: *prospective Buyers investigated the market longevity of products and parts being manufactured.*

As mentioned earlier, one of the very first questions I ask a prospective Seller is, "Why do you want to sell your business?"

When someone answers by telling me that they are NOT willing *to invest the required capital to update their product(s) in order to continue competing in the marketplace, my antenna goes up.*

My next question is "How much capital investment will be required to *keep sales revenues at recent and current levels?*"

The answer to that question will have a direct bearing on the valuation and marketability of the business.

> **EXAMPLE:** *Dual Processor, Inc. manufactures and assembles a first-generation dual microprocessor unit that has been sold to numerous automotive manufacturers for use in fuel injection and other electronic systems. However, computer industry engineers have been perfecting a new second-generation microprocessor. The new design will eventually be in high demand, replacing the first-generation processor units. This situation will substantially decrease demand for the original processor components within two years.*
>
> *The owners of Dual Processor, Inc. have determined that the company would need to spend $850,000 to re-tool its operations in order to produce the new units. The family board of directors has decided that instead of borrowing and investing $850,000, they will sell the business while the company is still profitable, enabling the shareholders to retire. Their plan is to reap the value of their company, and then let somebody else invest the capital required to keep the operations up to date.*

Based upon the facts presented in this example, *who do you think is actually going to end up paying the $850,000 (or more) for updating the company's operations?*

If you answered "the shareholders of Dual Processor, Inc.," then you would be correct. Why? If the current owners don't make the investment, then potential Buyers will *reduce their offer price to compensate for the needed capital expenditures*. The Sellers may then not have enough to retire.

When determining a purchase price, the prospective Buyers of Dual Processor will consider two scenarios: 1) what levels will revenues and profits decline without required additional investment in the business additional to the purchase price, and 2) if an $850,000 investment is made in the business in order to maintain historical revenues, how will that retooling investment impact future operating cash flows (after considering debt service and or return on the investment)?

The past performance of the company is analyzed by prospective Buyers to determine how likely the past will affect the future, either in a positive or negative way. A key point to always keep in mind: **Buyers purchase a business because of anticipated future earnings.** However, **they will pay for only what the company has done, or is doing currently.** If there is indication that the current level of revenue cannot be sustained, the value of the business will be negatively impacted.

My advice to business Sellers is this: projected declines in future revenue streams will cost the Seller in decreased business value. Compare cost associated with protecting or increasing revenue streams—verses possible decreased business value.

Buggy Whips and the Commodore 64

My father was born in 1912, and in less than one century he witnessed some of the most rapid technological advances known to man. I remember how he laughed as he reminisced about the "old timers" who rejected the notion that horses would be replaced as a means of transportation. He shared stories about how farmers in the "old days" had to hitch their teams of horses up to pull the mail carriers' Model Ts through the muddy rural roads. Who would have thought that modern technologies would overtake the noble horse?

During the nineteenth and early twentieth century saddle-making, harness making and the production of buggy whips were all thriving businesses. But times were changing. With the advent of the automobile, demand for a different type of product grew. Accordingly, technologies changed. Successful manufacturers invested capital in research and development projects, enabling forward-thinking manufacturers to supply the demand for more technologically advanced products.

In my own time, I remember being amazed at the development and marketing of the Commodore 64—one of the most technologically advanced gaming systems the world had ever seen (at that time). Amazingly that technology can't hold a candle to today's I-Pad and similar technologies.

One thing never changes: *there will always be change.* In order to maintain and grow business values, wise business owners will understand that continued reinvestment in technological advances is always necessary to maintain and grow business value.

> **Insider Tip:** *The business owners who think they will wait and let the next business owner invest in current technologies usually pays a dear price; most Buyers will discount their offer price by much more than the actual cost of the updated technologies.*

Outdated Information and Operating Technologies

Information Technologies

In this chapter we will address the need for up-to-date Information and Operating technologies.

Websites have become commonplace in today's business world. Yet we still find businesses that have no web presence. Or they have a very outdated website.

Today's business Buyers are technologically savvy, often performing web searches to learn about specific businesses in which they have an interest. A company that does not have web presence is sending a strong negative message about the company. R*emember, a Buyer's perception is just as important as the financial information about the business.*

A company having an *outdated* website may be viewed a bit more favorably than a company without any web presence at all depending on the prospective Buyer.

Websites are no longer just electronic business cards. Websites can be interactive, providing a great deal more information to potential customers. In many cases, websites can handle requests for quotes, provide information on available inventories, and even provide point-of-sale capabilities. Companies without updated web presence are perceived to be technologically inferior. Accordingly, a Buyer will factor this inferiority into any offer to purchase.

Owners should consider investing in updating their web presence before placing the company on the market. I am not suggesting that every business owner invest in a top of the line website, I am however, suggesting that at minimum, the information on the site is kept up to date, i.e., product lists, services etc.. In addition owners need to check out competitor's websites. You can be sure that potential Buyers will.

Remember, an investment in developing a site and keeping it updated is usually very small compared to the potential loss of value that could be incurred.

Operating Technologies

I would estimate that at least 99% of the time a company with technologically outdated production equipment won't be sold for what the owner believes his company is worth. We live in a technological society. Business owners who don't keep up with technology will be left behind in the dust.

A few years ago, I was visiting a business owner who produced hardwood parts for furniture and caskets. As we walked on the shop floor, the first thing I noticed was a mammoth piece of equipment covered with a plastic tarp. The tarp was covered by about four inches of sawdust and other debris. It was obvious to me that the machine hadn't been used for quite some time.

"That machine alone is worth $350,000!" the owner proclaimed.

"What is it and what does it do?" I asked.

"It's an old-fashioned 36-inch spindle lathe. It can turn a 30-foot by 36-inch diameter solid wood decorative column. You won't find too many of these anymore," he explained. "It takes a real craftsman to operate one of these babies."

The machine wasn't producing anything, and hadn't for quite some time. It had been built before the advent of computer-controlled equipment, and the company had no current or projected use for it.

The owner was a bit perturbed when I suggested he get rid of it. I explained that it added absolutely nothing to the value of the company. In fact, in my opinion, it detracted from the company's value. It was taking up valuable floor space, and every potential Buyer touring the plant would wonder the same thing: "How much will it cost to remove and dispose of that old monster?"

In the best-case scenario, if the owner thought the machine had value but not for his company, he might have sold it for scrap, or hired a salvage company to remove and haul the machine.

The business owner chose not to take my advice. The ultimate business acquirer told the Seller that he (the Seller) could just keep the old lathe so long as it was removed from the shop by the closing date. The Seller opted to take twenty thousand dollars less and leave the outdated equipment in place for the Buyer to deal with.

Some business owners lose sight of the fact that Buyers aren't impressed by the quantity of equipment on the floor. What impresses Buyers is **productive** and technologically capable machines and equipment.

> **Insider Tip:** *Removing outdated equipment and (in certain situations) replacing it with adequate equipment is strongly advised. It can pay off in the price you receive for your business.*

Exception to the Rule

As with every rule, there can be the occasional exception. Occasionally we come across a manufacturer who operates in a niche market where the outdated equipment is necessary. Often these companies are "survivors" in the sense that their competitors (who also didn't invest in modern technologies) are all out of business.

> **One example** *is a sand cast aluminum foundry we recently sold. Normally a company operating with such antiquated equipment couldn't be sold. But this company specialized in pouring very small orders for many unique parts that could not be economically produced in China. The customers didn't need hundreds of thousands of parts produced at one time (nor could they afford the shipping costs to bring the parts back across the water). This company's equipment could produce the volumes being requested by customers; it was more than adequate to meet significantly expanded demand for product. The Seller saw no reason to invest in newer equipment, and neither did the person who bought the company.*

With lean and "just-in-time" inventory deliveries, this foundry found a niche with dozens of different companies that needed smaller quantities of quality cast parts.

The most beautiful thing about the company was that they could get a **very** profitable "per-piece" price for everything they produced. The company sold because of the continuing demand for what they produced AND because the company would continue to be profitable using the older equipment in the future.

> **Another example** *of the "exception to the rule" was a machine tool company we sold a few years back. No CNC (computer controlled machine) technologies were to be found in this 20,000 square foot shop! There were eight skilled employees; the average age was 53. This team of machinists knew how to use the machines that were built in the 1940s, 50s, 60s and 70s (which has become a lost art with younger machinists).*
>
> *The Buyer of the company was a 40-year-old machinist who had interest in learning how to efficiently operate the old-style machines. The company sold because it had (in addition to several local customers) a dozen internationally known customers who demanded timely delivery of one- and two-part runs. The company could charge several times the "normal" price for each part. This was because 1) the shop catered to timely service, 2) the product quality was extremely high, and 3) the company distinguished itself by offering to provide service and delivery of a product that could not be found elsewhere.*

But again, keep in mind that this company was a survivor. It had lost hundreds of thousands of dollars before all competitors (who didn't reinvest in new technologies) were out of business. Once the competitors were gone, this company was able to dig through the rubble to establish its profitable niche.

In the two cases discussed, the companies were able to sell because they had survived economic downturns, and went on to carve out a niche for themselves. The new positioning allowed them to be profitable. Profitability is what sold the businesses.

Waiting on the Next Owner

Often companies don't invest in upgrading technologies because they may think that the next owner can make the investment. But most often, the next owners (the marketplace in general) will calculate the cost of technology upgrades—and discount the purchase price they offer to the Seller. In that case, who actually pays for the upgrades? The Seller pays because the price received is lower.

Best Advice

When the time to sell rolls around, do you want your prospective Buyers to learn about your company's competitive disadvantages? This situation can also produce the "double whammy" effect:

1. Your company may not have been as profitable as the companies of your peers because you did not possess the latest technologies; you may have lost some customers due to price competition, and the profits on your produced products may not have been as great as they could have been with the newer technologies.

2. In addition to the lost profits, your company will have also lost value. Remember the price multiplier scenario. If your type of company sells for 4 times EBITDA and your EBITDA is lower by $100,000 because of lost customers and lost profits, then you have also lost approximately $400,000 in business value!

In the "double whammy" scenario, one should consider the value of lost profits AND lost business value. Continuing to invest in productive technologies will pay dividends in many ways.

> **Insider Tip:** *Keep operating your company as if you were going to own and operate it forever. Even if you know you want to sell your company in a year or two don't neglect the technology upgrades that are common in your industry. If your competitors are all going to the next level of robotic automation in order to cut production costs and increase profitability, they may become more competitive than your company.*

Outdated Bookkeeping/Accounting Systems

Outdated bookkeeping and accounting systems can greatly devalue a business. Yet we continue to find environments of all sizes that are using some type of hand-posted journals and ledgers. Most of these companies will periodically send the rudimentary bookkeeping records to their CPA. The CPA will perform accounting functions and prepare a financial statement for the business owners. In some cases, the CPA does not prepare financial statements, but only prepares the tax returns at year end. *(This is the way things were done in the good old days.)* Many times systems are not updated because of the old adage "If it ain't broke, don't fix it." If it is not a direct cost of operations, why spend the money and time to update? Or sometimes the by-hand bookkeeper has been there forever and a day and is resistant to change.

Those good old days are gone forever. Today's business environment is fast paced and ever changing. Most Buyers will discount a company that employs antiquated bookkeeping and accounting systems because:

- Hand-written records can be hard to read and decipher (causing Buyer's due diligence to take longer and cost more)
- Hand-written journals and ledgers are not as easily analyzed as the computerized counterparts, and can contain more errors and other hidden issues
- Financial statements prepared by off-site CPAs are usually not prepared timely; they are not able to report the most up-to-date financial history (i.e., a day-to-day financial situation)
- The Buyers recognize that the old systems of bookkeeping will need to be updated into a modern computer-based system…and that costs time and money
- The Buyers tend to "pad" prospective costs of hardware, software, training and converting old data onto a new system. If $50,000 is the anticipated cost, most Buyers will double that cost to $100,000 to hedge for surprises. *The estimated conversion costs are always deducted from the sales price calculations*

Poorly Prepared Financial Statements

The appearance of your company's financial statements is very important. Poorly prepared financial statements that are obviously not computer generated and/or not prepared according to financial reporting standards can be a real *value-killer* for any business.

As we have discussed before, financial statements of private companies are typically prepared using accounting methods that minimize a company's taxable net income. This tends to be at odds with what a business owner wants to show to a potential Buyer in the context of a business sale. The goal, when presenting financial information to a potential acquirer, is to maximize the presentation of net income and cash flow. Since the primary factor influencing a company's value is its earnings, it is imperative to maximize the presentation of the financials.

Potential Buyers must be able to appreciate the actual cash flow or income-generating capability of the business. This can be achieved by starting with clear, concise, and descriptive financial statements. (It also helps if the data reflected on the financial statements was generated by up-to-date technologies.)

Ultimately, your financial statements will be *recast* or adjusted to reflect the discretionary economic benefits available to a new owner. The perceived ease of following the financial statement adjustments will make an impression upon the Buyer. If he sees you jumping through antiquated hoops to come up with the numbers, he may doubt your numbers. This in turn may affect the company's perceived value. *Remember, your business is competing with other similar businesses that Buyers are considering.*

Labor Union Contracts

There is no question in my mind about this: businesses with labor unions have a disadvantage when it comes time to sell the business. Many Buyers today aren't keen on having to deal with unions.

However, if your work-force is unionized, there are a couple of things you need to consider when trying to sell your business.

Potential business Buyers will want to see:

- Most recent union contract
- Copy of union contract that preceded the current contract
- Details of union complaints
- Details of union disputes
- Details of union strikes
- Details about company contributions to health, welfare and retirement benefits
- Details about other assessments for which the company is (or may be) liable
- Copies of letters from attorneys regarding union issues
- Details about expiration of current contract and prospects for next contract

> **Insider Tip:** *Labor law is very complex. If you are considering the sale of your business, I would strongly urge you to discuss the matter with your company's labor attorneys before getting deeply involved with a sale. In some cases there may be reporting and notification requirements before a sale can be pursued. Taking the precaution of obtaining legal advice first will be the safest bet.*

High Employee Turnover

Unless your business is seasonal in nature, high employee turnover is perceived by the marketplace as a very negative factor. This situation tends to decrease the offer a Buyer may be willing to make for your business.

Business Buyers will investigate (in the due diligence process) employees' employment history with your company. If a majority of your workforce has been with the company for several years, then that is a positive factor when price is considered.

In the event there are reasonable explanations for the high employee turnover, be ready and able to provide details.

The most important thing to remember about a history of high employee turnover is *whether or not the new owners will inherit the situations that caused the high rate of turnover.* In other words, has the problem been fixed?

What does Employee Turnover Cost?

The cost of losing key employees can be very high. It is important for companies to understand that general turnover rates in the workforce may also have a serious impact on a company's profitability and value.

There are a number of costs incurred as a result of employee turnover. A few of these are listed below.

1. The cost of lost opportunities while recruiting replacements. While the open position exists, what are the lost profits that might be associated with the position?

2. Administrative expenses which include advertising, screening and interviewing, security checks, credit reports, processing of references, and administering new hire testing.

3. Lost productivity due to the time required for a new worker to get up to speed on the job.

4. Lost productivity associated with the time that coworkers spend away from their own work to help a new worker.

5. Public relations costs associated with having a number of voluntary or involuntary terminations in the community (e.g., spreading gossip about the company).

6. The potential for increased unemployment insurance costs.

The foregoing factors must be considered when determining the substantial costs that can be associated with turnover.

Any prospective Buyer will consider whether or not those costs have already been incurred by the present owner (the Seller); or will the Buyer (new ownership) incur those costs? Accordingly, the potential Buyer will discount the price they will offer for your business.

The Causes of Turnover

There are numerous factors leading to employee turnover. Some of the factors are beyond the control of the employer. Some are not.

1. **The Economy**—one common reason given for leaving employment is the availability of higher paying jobs. In a poor economy, a matter of twenty-five cents per hour may cause some employees to leave. In a better economy the availability of alternative jobs when an employee becomes dissatisfied may play a part in employee turnover.

2. **The Performance of the Company** – a company that employees perceive to be in financial difficulty can also raise employee speculation about impending layoffs. Workers often think that it is rational to seek employment elsewhere before perceived layoffs.

3. **The Company's Culture**—It is important to understand that the reward system, the personality and strength of leadership, management's ability to inspire pride and commitment in the employee's, and instilling a sense of shared goals will influence employees' perceptions of their jobs. This all translates into the level of

job satisfaction among employees. Job satisfaction impacts the employee turnover rate.

4. **Job Characteristics**—Some jobs are more attractive than others. A job's perceived attractiveness can be influenced by many factors, including repetitiveness, challenge, danger, perceived importance, and capacity to achieve a sense of accomplishment.

5. **Unrealistic Expectations**—Unrealistic expectations that many employees have about their jobs can be a major issue. When unrealistic expectations are not realized, the employee can become disillusioned and decide to quit.

6. **The Person**—Personal factors, such as changes in family situations or an employee's desire to learn a new skill or trade, may influence an employee's decision to change jobs. Personal traits may be a predictor of job performance. Counterproductive behaviors such as loafing, absenteeism, theft, substance abuse on the job, and sabotage of employer's equipment or production might be determined by proper job screening to identify individuals' propensities for certain behaviors.

People who are satisfied with their jobs and who are committed to their employers are more likely to stay than those who are not. Prospective Buyers for your company are not just purchasing your inventory, equipment, and customer lists. A majority of Buyers want to acquire a trained and effective workforce! Buyers do not want to pay twice for a stable workforce (once in the purchase price of the business and again in hiring and replacement costs).

> **Insider Tip:** *By strengthening your workforce you are supporting the company's future revenue streams. This, in turn, converts to higher perceived value.*

Environmental Issues

The power of the Environmental Protection Agency (EPA) has grown considerably over the past several years. Working environments we once took for granted are now subject to even more regulations.

> **Insider Tip:** *Lenders frequently require environmental inspections of operating facilities, even when the facilities are going to be leased (and not purchased) by the new business owner.*

When "Clean" Might be "Dirty"

> **EXAMPLE:** *A few years ago we sold a commercial building maintenance company. The company provided basic janitorial cleaning services for banks, schools, hospitals, churches, offices, etc.. This company operated out of a 3,500 square foot building which was owned by a related party. The building was not going to be sold, but rather, leased to the purchasers of the business.*
>
> *The lender demanded an environmental survey of the business operation because of the cleaning products used by the company. The theory was that the cleaning agents had been stored in the building...and might have been spilled, causing an ongoing environmental problem. The Sellers had to cough up $1,100 for the environmental survey of the business.*
>
> *Fortunately the surveyor did not find chemical spills. They did, however, find that the heating and water pipe insulation contained asbestos. Luckily no action or clean-up was required.*

The preceding example turned out well for the Seller and there were not any cleanup costs to deal with. But, *had there been environmental findings,* the lender would **not have approved the bank loan** for the purchase of the business, unless and until the clean-up had been completed. If a clean-up would have been required, the sale might have been postponed or cancelled altogether depending upon the over-all cost and the time it would take for the clean-up.

All that Shines is not Aluminum!

> **EXAMPLE:** We represented an aluminum foundry business not too long ago. If you've been in a foundry, you know it is not a spotless place to work. Black soot and dust are found everywhere. When I questioned the Seller about environmental issues, he swore up and down the site was environmentally clean. No chemicals, and no dumped waste, etc..
>
> I asked how the company disposed of excess aluminum findings and grindings. The Seller told me that the company recycles everything. He said that he'd be willing to bet his last dollar that the site was environmentally clean. I told the Seller that a Buyer's lender would require a survey and if anything was found, he (the Seller) would pay for the clean-up. Plus, there was a chance of losing the deal if there were reported findings. I suggested that the Seller have a preemptive Phase I survey prepared. The Seller didn't want to spend the money.
>
> You are familiar with Murphy's Law. What can go wrong often does go wrong. The Buyer made an offer subject to contingencies (which included environmental contingencies). Sure enough, the lender needed a Phase I environmental survey. The surveyor learned that back in 1912 there had been petroleum storage tanks **on the next-door property** (which wasn't owned by the Seller). The storage tanks had been demolished in the 1930s. But, according to the environmental engineer, hydrocarbons might have leached onto the Seller's property.
>
> The environmental engineer called for a Phase II survey, which involved drilling core samples. This Phase II cost at that time was about $6,000. The Seller was "hot" to say the least. I reminded him that he should not have been surprised, as this has become common practice.
>
> The good news was that there were no hydrocarbon issues. The bad news: soil samples taken from around the old water well contained high concentrations of aluminum. How could that be?
>
> "Oh, yeah, I forgot," the Seller said with a sheepish grin. "We get rid of the unusable stuff by dumping it down the old well shaft! We just figured we'd fill the old shaft up and nobody would care."

The clean-up (removing dirt around the shallow well) cost about $2,500 and didn't take too long. The Seller paid the costs. The Buyer and the banker were happy and the deal closed. In this case, the sale closed after some pretty good bumps. Needless to say, both the lender and the Buyer could have pulled out at any time or renegotiated the price.

What You Can Do

If you are thinking about the sale of your business, you would do well to discover any environmental issues before placing the business for sale. It will save time, money, and possible embarrassment down the road by disclosing environmental issues up front. Also, in certain cases, having a preemptive environmental survey showing that the business is "clean" can be an effective sales tool when talking with prospective Buyers.

Safety Issues

OSHA stands for the Occupational Safety and Health Act of 1970. While well-intentioned, it is another one of the federal government's monster agencies that can make it difficult to be productive in smaller businesses.

Congress created the <u>Occupational Safety and Health Administration (OSHA)</u> to assure safe and healthy working conditions for men and women by setting and enforcing standards.

Any potential Buyer of your business will be interested in your company's OSHA experience history. If your company has had OSHA investigations and penalties, it is best to document the complete history and to show how you resolved each issue. Just as important is to show that your company continues to be in compliance with any adverse findings.

Insider Tip: *Buyers are risk adverse. If a potential Buyer suspects there are unresolved issues, the Buyer will associate possible future corrective costs with you, the current owner of the business. Again, expect this perception to have a negative impact on the value of your business. By showing that corrective actions have already been taken, you can reduce the Buyer's perceived risks and thus bolster the value of your company.*

Regulatory Issues

When preparing your business for sale, you need to have ready the answers to the following questions:

1. Have there been any Internal Revenue Service Audits? *The results of an IRS audit may change historical earnings. If the earnings went up, the good news is that fact might reflect positively on the company's earnings history.*

2. Have there been any State Tax Audits?

3. Have there been any Local Tax Audits?

4. Have licenses or permits been revoked anytime within the last 5 years?

5. Have there been audits by the State Workers' Compensation Commission or other governmental agencies?

6. Is the company registered to operate in each state that it has nexus, or in which it does business?

7. Are there currently, or have there been, zoning issues concerning the business location?

8. Have there been adverse inspections by the State Fire Marshall's Office?

Remember it's better to disclose up front (even if it seems meaningless to you) any issue that might come up during the due diligence, both positive and negative. Being able to show that the company has been checked for, and has passed (or corrected findings) on regulatory issues, can be a significant sales tool.

Of course, the flip side is also true, if you haven't taken care of regulatory issues, the Buyer will consider those issues in determining the price he is willing to pay for the business and whether or not to pursue the purchase of your business.

Customer Concentration Issues

By this time in your reading, I am sure you have gotten the message that *business Buyers are all risk adverse*. Some are more so than others. But there is one situation that will make Buyers cringe: *customer concentrations.*

When more than 10% of revenues come from one customer or when more than 25% of revenues come from the top five customers, then *customer concentration is an issue with potential business Buyers; it can be a potential show stopper.*

This situation creates numerous concerns. The biggest one is that only one or two unfavorable decisions from a major customer can turn your business from being profitable to unprofitable. And, from a Buyers' viewpoint, this situation becomes much more likely after the Seller leaves the business

Remember the previous *risk* discussions? *The higher the perceived risks—the lower the offering price.* Buyers will typically discount the amount they are willing to pay for a business with high customer concentration by 30-50%. What's even worse? If the customer concentration is too high, many Buyers decide not to make an offer at all.

Sellers who face this issue should strive to invest the time and money to increase the overall number of customers and to find ways to increase the revenues to current customers.

Can You Hear Me Now?

One of our clients operated an extremely profitable engraving and plastic injection molding company. The company specialized in building tools for injection molding for arthroscopic surgery devices. Revenues were in excess of $8 million per year; their EBITDA was consistently 30% of revenues ($2,400,000). Their dilemma: $7.5 million of the revenue came from one customer! If this one customer left, the company could have been ruined. The owners of the company prepared a brochure that highlighted the company's abilities. These brochures were sent (both electronically and physically) to other distributors of medical type equipment. Within a few months, two of the world's largest manufacturers of hearing aid devices contacted them. Soon thereafter the company began building tools and injecting parts for both of the hearing aid manufacturers. Later, other medical related manufacturers and distributors also became customers. The company has a significant new market segment using the technologies and products that they already knew how to produce. This situation improved value as it was perceived by the outside market.

> **Insider Tip:** *Consider marketing an existing product/service to a new market. Be creative!*

Industry Concentration Issues

The concern about *industry concentrations* within your business is similar to *customer concentration* issues. If your customers are heavily concentrated in one industry, risk to the Buyer is perceived to be great. The greater the perceived risks—the lower the perceived value of your company.

> **EXAMPLE:** *Ajax Widgets Company manufactures numerous types of plastic injection molded parts for the automobile industry. Their customers include a dozen OEM manufacturers and over a dozen after market customers. Ajax has annual revenues of $20 million per year, with EBITDA of $3 million. While this is a profitable company with a very good EBITDA to Sales ratio, many Buyers will see this glass as being half empty! Why? 100% of the Ajax revenues are derived from the automotive industry. Buyers reason that a significant downturn in the automotive industry could have a catastrophic effect on Ajax.*

Up until 2007 the U.S. auto industry seemed to be motoring along fine. But then in 2008, market conditions began to drastically change. 2009 was the absolute bottom for most automotive parts manufacturers and many didn't survive.

The parts manufacturers *who did survive* all had one thing in common: they had customers in industries other than automotive to fall back on.

Many of the clients I worked with during the automotive downturn derived 28 to 32 percent of their total revenues (up through 2007) from consumer goods, medical products, and *other non-automotive industries*. When the automotive market crash occurred, the non-automotive revenues and profits were significant enough to maintain the businesses.

> **Insider Tip:** *A company with more than 50% of its business concentration in one industry may not be the pariah feared by most Buyers.* **But there is a trick to this scenario.** *The profits derived from the minority industry concentrations must be more than enough to pay the company's fixed overhead in the absence of the heavily concentrated business.*

If your company is heavily concentrated in one industry, it would be wise to secure work within other industries as well. Even diversifying within different segments of the same industry can reduce some of the perceived risks.

> **EXAMPLE:** *We worked with a client who derived 90% of their revenues from molding and assembling parts for the prosthetic limb industry. The client faced the possibility that American suppliers would eventually turn to offshore manufacturers. I suggested that the company broaden its industry and customer bases. Due to their efforts, the company landed a couple of large customers who specialized in manufacture and assembly of electronic nerve stimulation units. One of the customers was domestic and one was foreign. Ostensibly, the company was still concentrated in the medical field. But the diversity within the medical field might disperse some Buyers' aversions to the industry risk exposure.*

While diversifying revenues among several industries is good advice, it is much easier said than done. But *any gains* made in expanding your business into other profitable industry opportunities would be a step in the right direction.

Competitive Pressures

I remember back in the late 1970s when a Domino's Pizza shop first opened in our city. It was one of just four pizza shops in our county. The pizza business was the mother-load, according to some of the independent store owners I knew; everybody in the pizza business was making a bundle of money.

Good News Travels Fast

Good news about profitable business opportunities travels fast! The Domino's franchise owners opened three more locations in our county. Pizza Hut opened a store, and then a second store. Little Caesars Pizza, Godfather Pizza, East of Chicago Pizza, and a whole host of other non-franchise shops opened. Entrepreneurs everywhere wanted to cash in on the pizza bonanza. Pizza could be purchased on almost every street corner (a slight exaggeration)!

Today many of those pizza shops in our area are no longer operating. They just couldn't remain competitive and profitable enough to keep the lights on.

The surviving pizza shops endlessly promote pizza bargains. Turn on the television and you are bound to see pizza advertisements. Open your newspaper and a pizza sale flyer falls to the floor. Try to use the internet and "pop-up" pizza ads flash before your eyes! Some of the pizza advertisers are literally giving pizzas away just to get you to order from them!

How can a pizza shop make money selling large single-item pizzas for $4? The answer is: some of them aren't making much money at all. Franchise owners can seldom survive on the profits generated by only one location; they need to own multiple locations and run very lean operations to make decent profits.

It's fair to say that the hay days of the pizza shop industry are long gone. This can all be attributed to competition. Competition is good for consumers because customers benefit from lower prices. But competition can be a tough nut to crack for the business owner.

One way to "crack the competition nut" is the continued improvement of existing products and the development of new product (that competitors don't have). You will notice that the national food chains are constantly releasing new product offerings. This gets back to the following core value principle:

A Unique Core Differentiator. Also known as a Unique Selling Proposition, a Unique Core Differentiator (UCD) is a means of differentiating a business from its competitors. Having a UCD means that the business *may be less dependent on pricing* as a strategy for growing its business. A UCD might be the way a business packages its products or services, or the way it promotes itself in a way its competitors cannot match.

Pizza connoisseurs might think that some famous pizza chef somewhere had a flash of genius when he or she figured out that putting pineapple on pizza tasted good. That may be true. But my bet is that the pizza chef was dabbling with new recipes in order to offer something to customers that no other pizza shop had. The pineapple pizza became a unique selling proposition—until every pizza shop in North America caught on to the concept.

Combating Competitive Pressures

Businesses that survive a tough competitive environment do so because they find new technologies to make their products better, faster, and less costly. Using the pizza industry as an example:

- Pizza entrepreneurs have cut labor costs by developing ovens that are built over timed pizza conveyors
- Automated robotic oven loading and unloading equipment (reducing labor costs)
- Perfecting "JIT" (just-in-time) inventory deliveries
- Automated telephone order-taking capabilities thus streamlining the ordering process while cutting labor costs
- Online ordering and credit card payment systems
- Advertising and promotions have expanded to cyber technologies

The preceding example demonstrates how the highly competitive pizza business environment has changed the way that *entire industry* operates.

If a business Buyer considers the purchase of a business in any industry, a comprehensive analysis of competitive pressures within the industry, and those facing the specific business, will be made.

The more competition a business has, the greater the risk factors associated with that business. As risk increases, *perceived value decreases*.

In a *highly competitive industry*, business operators realize that in order to survive, they must *out-maneuver* their competition. Future cash flows from the business will be needed for:

- Demographic studies to determine where customers are
- Determining customers' capacity to buy
- Determining what the customers want and need
- Research and development to produce newer and better products and services
- Capital expenditures for innovation and modernization of equipment and operating systems

- Continuing advertising campaigns to maintain
- New advertising campaigns to promote the newly-developed products and services

Is your business in a highly competitive industry or market? No matter what industry your business is in, potential Buyers will consider how much of your businesses future cash flow will be needed to survive in your particular business environment. You can combat competitive pressure by developing and/or implementing new techniques and improved technologies to better deliver your products and services.

Appearances

The appearance of your business has a direct impact upon the value of your business. A shabby business exterior does not leave favorable impressions with employees, customers, or potential purchasers of your business.

The same is true for the interior of the business. If appearances portray disarray and unkemptness, the perceived value of the business will be negatively impacted.

> **EXAMPLE:** *Suppose you are in the market for a new car. You go to the dealer's lot and see two identical cars sitting on the lot—same mileage and the exact make, model, and color you had in mind. Identical in every aspect except one needs to be prepped and cleaned up. The other is spotless. Which one draws your attention? At that very moment, which car has the greatest appeal? Some Buyers might think, well, I can buy the less attractive vehicle for less money. That sentiment proves my point. Something less attractive is perceived to be worth less money. Granted, a business is not an automobile. But the perception of "worth" works much the same, whether buying a car, home, or business.*

Keep your business establishment well groomed, inside and out. A well-maintained appearance may go a very long way in keeping the public's perception that yours is a top notch business. You never know when the next best customer or even business Buyer may come through the door.

Other Important Considerations

In this chapter, I want to share with you a few additional considerations as you prepare your business for sale.

Choosing the Wrong Time to Sell

It's very common for business owners to spend all of their efforts building their business and doing very little along the way to *prepare their company for its eventual sale.* As an owner you might be telling yourself that when it's time to move on to greener pastures you'll simply put the company on the market.

However, just because *you are ready to sell the business* doesn't mean the business is in a position to command an attractive price. *If the company's growth, profits and cash flows aren't optimal,* you stand to leave a significant amount of value (your money) on the table. *Plus,* if you time your sale when credit and capital markets aren't receptive to acquisitions, your pool of potential acquirers might be diminished.

The best approach is to get your company prepared today for its eventual sale. Make some of the suggestions in this guide part of your daily operating procedures. This way you can sell with little preparation time when market conditions are most favorable.

Failing to Hire Experienced Advisors

Selling your business is a complex process. There are very few, if any, business owners who have the expertise to navigate the legal and financial details of a sale. Can you sell it yourself? Maybe yes, but I can pretty much guarantee you won't leave the table with the best price! You need a team to help you make informed decisions and to keep the sale on track. Remember, selling your business is not something you should take for granted. A successful sale that will meet your expectations takes careful planning and a great deal of expertise.

Your team should be comprised of:

Accountants who are familiar with your business. If you have not used a Certified Public Accounting (CPA) firm in the past, you need to think about using one.

Certified Public Accountants are licensed and have to stick to strict guidelines in preparing reports. When presenting financial statements not prepared or screened by CPAs, the Buyer may perceive that the books are incorrect. Be aware that a Buyer may require, as part of a deal, to have the books reviewed by an agreed-upon CPA.

Tax Advisors. Some CPAs are also good tax advisors, and some are not. Make no mistake: knowing the income tax implications of selling your business is huge! Remember, it's not about the size of the sale price. *It is about how much you bring home after taxes!*

Don't make the mistake of waiting until you get an offer to purchase before you look at the income tax implications. It is best to work through different sale price scenarios and their tax implications before setting a price and going to market.

> **Insider Tip:** *Although you should work out beforehand the tax implications of a sale price, keep in mind there are many scenarios that may allow you to get to the after tax dollars amount you want to keep. In certain situations it may even be better to agree to a lower sale price! A good CPA and Business Intermediary (Business Broker) will be able to contribute ideas to put together a deal that meets or exceeds your after tax needs.*

Tax advisors *might* be CPAs, Enrolled Agents, or Attorneys at Law. It is best to interview the tax advisors to be certain that they routinely handle *business sales transactions*.

An Experienced Transaction Attorney. Many Sellers think that the attorney who did their incorporation papers or who prepared their will is qualified to handle the closing and deal-making for the sale of the business. While you may seek the advice of your family attorney or corporate attorney as the deal progresses, your best bet will be to hire a transaction attorney. Attorneys are like doctors. You wouldn't go to a proctologist to fix a broken arm (I hope!). Many obstacles will come up during and after a sale. You want to have the best advice from an attorney who has been at the closing table many times before. Also, an experienced transaction professional will save you attorney fees in the long run. If he or she has worked on many successful closings, he will not waste your money or time on his or her learning curve.

A Certified Business Intermediary (CBI). Without someone to guide a business sale transaction through the Buyer/Seller obstacle course, selling a business can easily become a three-ring circus. (This is not the time to be dealing with clowns.) It is not only a Certified Business Intermediary's job to market your business and find a Buyer, but also to keep the accountants, attorneys, and others moving toward your goal of selling the business for the best price and in a timely fashion. Keep in mind that not all business brokers are created equal. Look for a broker who has earned the CBI (Certified Business Intermediary) designation. A broker with the CBI designation adheres to a strict code of professional ethics. In order to earn the CBI designation, a candidate must earn prerequisite formal and industry education, obtain experience working in the business brokerage field, pass a written examination and is required to keep up to date with professional continuing education.

> **Insider Tip:** *Certified Business Intermediaries are experienced, trained, and tested to know how to confidentially bring business Buyers and business Sellers together. The CBI understands financial statements and knows how to be the expert liaison between Buyers, Sellers, attorneys, accountants, and lenders. In short, a CBI knows how to get a deal completed.*

A Wealth Management Specialist. Before selling your business, you may need to seek the advice of a wealth management specialist. Having some idea of how and where to invest the proceeds from selling your business is prudent financial planning. If you try to go it alone without the benefit of specialized expertise, you can place your post-business lifestyle at risk.

Also, arranging your personal finances for life after selling your business relieves some of the emotional stress that can accompany the sale of one's business.

Consider the Tax Implications of Your Sale

Income taxes can eat up a significant portion of the money you receive from the sale of your business. In fact, many Sellers are surprised by, and unprepared for, the size of their tax bills. By planning ahead and working with qualified tax professionals, you may be able to structure your deal to minimize the tax bite. Deal structures that provide tax relief for the Buyer usually impose higher taxes on the Seller, and vice versa.

Failing to understand the tax complexities of any deal most likely will place you in a disadvantageous financial position.

Have Your Company Appraised

Business owners should consider having their company expertly valued even if they are not planning to sell in the near future. Learning that the sale of your business won't properly fund your retirement when you are emotionally ready to sell might be a new low point in your life. When you know your situation up front, you will then have time to make corrections/changes in your business and/or adjust your personal investment plan and retirement expectations.

Plan in Advance

Whether you intend to sell in a year or in a decade, you need a plan in place now. Otherwise, when the time comes, you will find yourself *reacting to events rather than planning for and anticipating them.* The more you understand how the sale process works, the better your decisions will be.

> **Insider Tip:** *An exit plan allows you to recognize optimal market conditions and guide you through the sale process. It also takes some of the uncertainty out of your future. If you haven't already started putting a plan together, do it today. Otherwise, time will slip away from you, and along with it—your opportunity to achieve your goal of a comfortable retirement.*

Prepare for Buyer Due Diligence in Advance

Before someone closes on the purchase on your business, they and their accounting, legal, and lending teams will make an examination of your business. This process is called *due diligence.*

Remember a Buyer is new to you and your business. They try to leave no rock untouched in their examination of the business. Patience is the key to get the deal done and meet your goal of selling. The more you are prepared in advance the less painful the process will be.

> **Insider Tip:** *When a potential Buyer has interest in purchasing your business you need to be ready to provide (with guidance of your team) the information they request pretty darn quick. Buyers are fickle. If you haven't provided what they have reasonably requested within a short time, they may move on to another deal. Most likely the Buyer hasn't fallen in love with your business yet and will not want to deal with a Seller who isn't interested in providing what is needed in a timely fashion.*
>
> *You want to have everything ready the Buyer might need in advance of asking for it, but you need to allow your Business Broker to feed them the information in a controlled flow. The process of keeping a Buyer interested in pursuing your business is sort of like hooking a fish. "You want to feed the line out and pull" at just the right time or you can lose him!*

Preparing for the Process

You may not be thinking about selling your business today, but think about this; would **you** consider *buying* your business if you didn't already own it? You need to look at the business through the Buyer's eyes.

What issues might you discover that would frighten you away from the purchase of your business?

It is always good to review your own situation with impartiality. When was the last time you put your business under a microscope? Take an in-depth look at your business the way a purchaser will someday. An internal review may bring to light what steps you may need to take to get ready for a sale. The results of this exercise might surprise you!

Is Your Organization in Good Order?

Pretend you are the potential Buyer of your business. You'd like to learn as much about the business as possible in a relatively short period of time. Whether an eventual sales transaction is structured as an asset transaction, a stock transaction, or a merger, potential Buyers will want to know what they are getting into. They will require detailed information from the Seller (you) regarding business operations and finances.

The following is a partial checklist of information and documents you will likely be expected to address for the benefit of a Buyer. Pulling these items together ***before engaging with a Buyer is an excellent strategy***. Reviewing the documents before placing your company on the market will prevent you from making a last-minute discovery of something you totally forgot about and intended to fix prior to selling. Some discoveries may prove embarrassing and cost you creditability when dealing with a Buyer and his or her team.

Review the following items as they pertain to your business. These items should be ready to distribute to the Buyer's team as needed. Note: many of the following items will only be provided to Buyers who have submitted, and for which you have accepted, a Letter of Intent (LOI) or Contingent Purchase Offer (CPO). Your Business Broker and the rest of your team will direct you as to which items you will need to provide to the Buyer and when is the proper time.

Legal Information

- The company's articles of incorporation and all amendments. *Some business owners have lost track of these and need to get copies from their attorney*

- The company's bylaws and all amendments

- The company's minutes book, including all minutes and resolutions of shareholders and directors and executive committees. *It is not uncommon for companies to ignore updating their corporate minutes annually. This is very important to have completed, especially if any creditors attempt to pierce the corporate veil)*

- The company's organizational chart. *Only about half the companies we have worked with have had organizational charts, organizational charts are always requested for Buyer's due diligence procedures even if you are a small business*

- The company's list of shareholders and type and number of shares held by each

- Copies of agreements relating to options, voting trusts, warrants, puts, calls, subscriptions, and convertible securities

- A certificate of good standing from the secretary of state or states where the company is incorporated or registered to do business

- A list of all states where the company is authorized to do business and annual reports for the last three years. *Some companies transact business in other states, but are not authorized to do business in those states. This can present legal problems*

- A list of all states, provinces, or countries where the company owns or leases property, maintains employees, or conducts business

- A list of all of the company's assumed names and copies of registrations thereof

Financial Information

- Financial statements for at least the most recent three years, together with accountant's reports

- The most recent (year-to-date) financial statements, with comparable statements to the prior year

- The company's credit report, if available. *I suggest that every company obtain its own credit report at least once per year*

- Any projections, capital budgets, and strategic plans

- A schedule of all indebtedness and contingent liabilities. Contingent liabilities might include product warranties and guarantes, liabilities for unredeemed coupons, etc.)

- A schedule of recent inventory. *Most Sellers will have this as of the most recent year ended*

- A schedule of accounts receivable. *Most Sellers will have this as of the most recent year ended*

- A schedule of accounts payable. *Most Sellers will have this as of the most recent year ended*

- A description of the company's internal control procedures. *This is another item that many businesses do not have documented, or in force. It is not unheard of for smaller companies to fall victim to fraud and embezzlement. Having internal control procedures in place and documented adds some perceived value to any business*

Physical Assets

- A schedule of fixed assets and their locations

- All U.C.C. filings (liens on your assets)

- All leases of equipment

- A schedule of sales and purchases of major capital equipment during the last three years

Real Estate

- A schedule of the company's business locations

- Copies of all real estate leases, deeds, mortgages, title policies, surveys, zoning approvals, variances or use permits

Intellectual Property

- A schedule of domestic and foreign patents and patent applications
- A schedule of trademark and trade names
- A schedule of copyrights
- A description of important technical know-how (methods, procedures, processes)
- A description of methods used to protect trade secrets and know-how
- "work for hire" agreements
- A schedule and copies of all consulting agreements, agreements regarding inventions, and licenses or assignments of intellectual property to or from the company
- A schedule and summary of any claims or threatened claims by or against the company regarding intellectual property

Employees and Employee Benefits

- List of employees, positions, salaries, and bonuses paid during last three years, and years of service
- All employment, consulting, nondisclosure, non-solicitation or noncompetition agreements between the company and any of its employees
- Resumes of key employees
- The company's personnel handbook and a schedule of all employee benefits and holiday, vacation, and sick leave policies
- Summary plan descriptions of qualified and non-qualified retirement plans
- Copies of collective bargaining agreements, if any
- A description of all employee problems within the last three years, including

alleged wrongful termination, harassment, and discrimination

- A description of any labor disputes, requests for arbitration, or grievance procedures currently pending or settled within the last three years

- A list and description of benefits of all employee health and welfare insurance policies or self-funded arrangements

- A description of workers' compensation claims history

- A description of unemployment insurance claims history

- Copies of all stock option and stock purchase plans and a schedule of option grants

Licenses and Permits

- Copies of any governmental licenses, permits, or consents

- Any correspondence or documents relating to any proceedings of any regulatory agency

Environmental Issues

- Environmental audits, if any, for each property leased by the company

- A listing of hazardous substances used in the company's operations and where they are stored

- A description of the Company's disposal methods

- A list of environmental permits and licenses

- Copies of all correspondence, notices, and files related to EPA, state, or local regulatory agencies

- A list identifying and describing any environmental litigation or investigations

- A list identifying and describing any known superfund exposure
- A list identifying and describing any contingent environmental liabilities or continuing indemnification obligations

Taxes

- Federal, state, local, and foreign income tax returns for the last three years
- States sales tax returns for the last three years
- Any audit and revenue agency reports
- Any tax settlement documents for the last three years
- Employment tax filings for three years
- Excise tax filings for three years
- Any tax liens

Material Contracts

- A schedule of all subsidiary, partnership, or joint venture relationships and intercompany obligations, with copies of all related agreements
- Copies of all contracts between the company and any officers, directors, 5 percent shareholders, or affiliates
- All loan agreements, bank financing arrangements, line of credit, or promissory notes to which the company is a party
- All security agreements, mortgages, indentures, collateral pledges, and similar agreements
- All guaranties to which the company is a party
- Any installment sale agreements

- Any distribution agreements, sales representative agreements, marketing agreements, and supply agreements

- Any letters of intent, contracts, and closing transcripts from any mergers, acquisitions, or divestitures within the last five years

- Any options and stock purchase agreements involving interests in other companies

- The company's standard quote, purchase order, invoice and warranty forms

- All nondisclosure or noncompetition agreements to which the company is a party

- All other material contracts

Product or Service Lines

- A list of all existing products or services and products or services under development

- Copies of all correspondence and reports related to any regulatory approvals or disapprovals of any company's products or services

- A summary of all complaints or warranty claims

- A summary of results of all tests, evaluations, studies, surveys, and other data regarding existing products or services under development

Customer Information

- A schedule of the company's five largest customers in terms of sales thereto and a description of sales thereto over a period of at least two years

- Any supply or service agreements

- A description or copy of the company's purchasing policies

- A description or copy of the company's credit policy
- A schedule of unfilled orders
- A list and explanation for any major customers lost over the last two years
- All surveys and market research reports relevant to the company or its products or services
- The company's current advertising programs, marketing plans and budgets, and printed marketing materials
- A description of the company's major competitors

Litigation

- A schedule of all pending litigation
- A description of any threatened litigation
- History of past litigation
- Copies of insurance policies possibly providing coverage as to pending or threatened litigation
- Documents relating to any injunctions, consent decrees, or settlements to which the company is a party
- A list of unsatisfied judgments

Insurance Coverage

- A schedule and copies of the Company's general liability, personal and real property, product liability, errors and omissions, key-man, directors and officers, workers' compensation, and other insurance
- A schedule of the company's insurance claims history for the past three years

Professionals

- A schedule of all law firms, accounting firms, consulting firms, and similar professionals engaged by the company during past five years

Articles and Publicity

- Copies of all articles and press releases relating to the company within the past three years

Tackle Deal-killers Early On

In earlier sections we have mentioned *skeletons in the closet*. Skeletons in your business closet could jeopardize the sale of your business. Since these issues may eventually surface (and they usually do), it is far better to address them proactively rather than having to take a defensive posture when they are uncovered.

Many common deal-killers have already been mentioned in this guide. But, **here are a few more that I think are worth mentioning:**

- Expired patents that require attention
- Expired franchise agreements
- Expired royalty agreements
- Termination of favorable purchasing terms
- Leases that need to be renegotiated or renewed
- Workers' compensation claims that will affect future premium rates
- Financials needing revisions
- Pending litigation
- Expired non-compete agreements with employees
- Expired employee confidentiality agreements

Addressing these issues in a timely and forthright manner avoids spending months identifying qualified acquirers only to have your sale fall through because certain issues were not anticipated and addressed at the onset of Buyer due diligence.

Insider Tip: *Buyers will have a greater willingness to proceed when they feel the Seller has been honest in disclosing unattractive issues up front. The Buyer's perception is that you are being forthcoming and there are no hidden surprises.*

Conclusion

The secret to improving the value of your company isn't really a secret at all. It comes down to two basic tactics:

1. Enhance and showcase all the positive elements of your company.
2. Identify problem areas (risks) and reduce or eliminate them.

If you're like many business owners, you might think you have quite a bit of time before you sell or exit your company. But consider this: until recently* only 10% of privately owned companies are sold because of retirement. It has been estimated that 54% sell because of business owner burn-out: BOB (go to www.gruttercpas.com for a blog article about BOB Syndrome), 10% sell because of disability, 10% sell because of death. 16% sell for various other reasons. Unfortunately, you can't predict when you may feel burnt out, become disabled or when a devastating illness comes knocking at your door. Keep in mind how your day to day decisions may impact the eventual sale of your business.

* NOTE: *in 2012 an estimated 50% of business sales were due to retirement. As baby-boomers retire---a glut of businesses will come available for sale.*

As you contemplate the sale of your business, I invite you to contact me toll free at 1-866-825-VALUATE (8283). Or e-mail me at grutter@gruttercpas.com. I also urge you to review the Seller information section of our web site at www.gruttercpas.com. You are sure to find additional information that will assist you in preparing your business for sale to gain the highest possible price.

Planning Checklists

Checklist: Factors that Increase or Decrease the Value of Your Business

Item #	Increases Your Business Value	Decreases Your Business Value
1	Organized, up-to-date financial statements	Incomplete, inaccurate, untimely (out-of-date) financial statements
2	Modern computer and information systems with up-to-date versions of software	Hand-posted information systems or old / outdated computer hardware and software
3	Computer and information back-up and redundancy systems	Lack of timely information back-up and lack of IT systems redundancy
4	Provable, documented owner perks and benefits	Un-provable owner perks and benefits; decreasing owner perks
5	Increasing annual sales	Flat or decreasing annual sales
6	Reporting all sales and income items	Generating "under the table" and unproven cash income
7	Key people "in-place" and capable of operating business in owner's absence	Heavy reliance on owner to operate the business, handle customers, etc..
8	Operating systems in place and documented, updated	No documentation of "how things work" and who is responsible for certain functions
9	Organization charts	Lack of organizational charts

10	Well-defined sales methodology / strong sales force	No clearly defined method for generating revenues/or no sales force
11	Cross-trained employee base	Untrained or under-trained work force/high employee turn-over
12	Diverse long-term customer / client base in stable industries	Infrequent customers, non-returning customers, concentration and relying on only a few customers, relying on only one or two Industries
13	Intellectual property and or proprietary processes	No intellectual property, no unique proprietary processes, nothing that distinguishes the business product or services
14	Clean balance sheet: No non-business-related assets mixed in with business assets	Personal and other non-business assets (or unrelated business assets) Combined with business assets in the balance sheet
15	Good and visible location	Poor and hard to find location
16	Well designed website (may include sales and transaction capabilities)	No website, or old and dated website
17	Good appearance both exterior and interior	Poor curb appeal and unclean, un-organized shop and offices
18	Good reason for selling: retirement, health, (burnout can be acceptable reason), etc..	No definite reason for selling, Seller has no definitive post-sale plans
19	Newly designed, updated products/services with future demand	Older products/services that will be less in demand in the future
20	In compliance with federal, state and local regulations, etc..	Lack of compliance, or problems with compliance with federal, state and/or local regulations, etc..

Checklist: Does Your Company Have These Value-drivers?

Possible Value-driver	Description	How You Can Develop Yours
Positive Earnings Before Interest, Taxes, Depreciation and Amortization (EBITDA)	This is not profit, but rather the pre-tax profit plus interest expense, plus depreciation expense, plus amortization expense. Many smaller businesses and mid market businesses will sell for a multiple of EBITDA (from 1 x to 6 times).	Ask your CPA to add a supplemental schedule to your financial statements each year, showing the annual EBITDA of your business. In fact, ask the CPA to help you monitor and improve your company's EBIDTA from year to year. It you decide to do this you must take the time to be honest and accurate or your efforts will be wasted.
Excellent Customer List	Do you have well-known, large or unique clients or customers? Could your customers possibly be excellent customers for a potential Buyer wishing to make inroads with the customer?	Develop a comprehensive profile on each of your customers. In what industry do they operate? What products do they use other than yours? What is their financial strength? What are your customer's long term growth projections?
Product Differentiation	Does your company have a unique service? Products with particular qualities not possessed by the competition? Services or products that out-perform those of competitors? The only product of its type?	Within your company prospectus spend some time listing all of the benefits and unique characteristics of your company's products and services.
Defensible Market Positioning	This is a product, service or other intangible asset that cannot be easily replicated by another company (competitor). This could be a long-term	Develop a comprehensive profile of each defensible position and list all the benefits associated with the position. Can these positions be transferred to another owner? If

	association with a client, government contract, special licensing, patents, copyrights, trademarks, brand names, access to low-cost supplies, favorable terms with suppliers, favorable associations with vendors, etc..	not, can changes be made so they are? Develop an argument as to why these positions should be coveted by a potential owner.
Dominant Market Share	An extremely important driver is for the company to command a strong position within the market for its products and services.	Develop a statistical graph tracking the estimated total dollar volume of the market in which you operate, comparing the total to your dollar share of the market—and that of your competitors. This, if updated annually, is also a great visual tool for you and your management team. For example, auto dealers can get statistics on the number of autos sold and how many were sold by each dealer within a certain market. Funeral directors can get stats on the number of deaths within a market area, and the number of cases they handled. The same is true for obstetricians for the number of births. Some industries may not have information readily available, so the business owner should develop reasonable estimates of their company's market share.
Technology and Proprietary Processes	Proprietary technology doesn't necessarily have to be patented to be valuable. In some instances, such processes are highly confidential and carefully guarded. Once a prospective client took me on a tour of his family's facility. There was a huge machine covered by a large tarp which was securely fastened to the floor. He	If you own patents or copyrights, by all means update your company "prospectus" to describe these and highlight the positive aspects of owning them. If you have technology or processes that provide great economic or competitive benefits, you do not have to describe the processes in your prospectus—but definitely elaborate on the economic and

	explained what the machine could do. I was amazed. I mentioned that the patent on that machine must be worth a fortune! I was surprised when he told me they had never filed for a patent because nobody else could come close to doing what his machine did. And, because the machine allowed their business to be a leader in their industry, they were taking no chances on providing the drawings to the U.S. Patent office!	competitive advantages enjoyed by the company as a result of the ownership.
Location	Sometimes, a competitive advantage may be the location in which your business operates. If your company enjoys high visibility, is accessible, has good customer parking, is well lit, located in a low crime area, is in a favorable per-household income demographic, is under a favorable lease arrangement, etc.., these may all be value-drivers.	Have you documented the positive attributes of your location within your prospectus? Is this something that your business enjoys, but that your competitors do not enjoy? Do you enjoy favorable lease rates over a long period of time? Accentuate the positive things about your location!
Franchise/Dealership	Do you own a well known franchise or dealer operation that is successful?	Document the length of time remaining under the agreement, the benefits of owning the franchise and the advantages over the competition.

The foregoing table lists just a few of the *value-drivers* your company might possess. Your company may have additional and different value-drivers.

> **Insider Tip:** *Just like making a list of Pros and Cons—make a list of your company's Pros, its value-drivers. Work on adding to the list of value-drivers, and then improving each driver.*

Checklist: Possible Risks Associated with Your Business

When the time comes to sell your business, potential Buyers will perform "due diligence" procedures to determine all the risks associated with your business. Investors are risk adverse. The more perceived risk that is associated with an investment—the lower the value of the investment.

> **Insider Tip:** *Know the risks associated with your own company! The following table lists some possible problems about which you should be aware. Identifying your company's perceived risks should assist you in making corrections—thus increasing your company's value. In some instances, you may not be able to eliminate a risk, but you might be able to mitigate (reduce) the risk associated with the situation. In the event you should ever want (or need) to sell your business—reduced risks increase the price of your business.*

Risks	Mitigation Considerations	Check if This Situation Needs to be Addressed/Improved
Lawsuits for Prior Acts or Products Produced and Services Rendered in the Past	• What types of exposure does your company (and possibly a purchaser) face for prior acts, products and services? • Does your company have adequate insurance to cover certain types of liability associated with prior acts and products produced or services rendered in the past? Document and discuss your situation with your attorney. Document your attorney's response. If the legal opinion is that little or no exposure exists—document and keep the lawyer's opinion in your business prospectus. This will mitigate the perception of risk—and increase the value of your business to some degree. If your attorney suggests certain actions you should take—take those actions and document them.	
Loss of Customers	In the table for "value-drivers" I suggested you	

	discuss the primary customers of your business. A firm knowledge and understanding of your customers and clients can be easily transferred to a new owner—to make the new owner comfortable with the customer base. This documentation can go a long way to reduce risks that are perceived by a potential Buyer of your company.	
Outdated Technology, Products, etc..	If your product/service line and technology are up to date, those facts can be accentuated in the **value-driver** section of your prospectus. In the event your product/services and technologies need to be updated, address the company plans for making such updates, and the estimated capital required to accomplish the updates. List potential sources of capital for completing the updates.	
Labor Force/Employment Issues	<ul><li>Is there a union in the workplace?</li><li>If not, what is the potential for the workforce installing a union?</li><li>What are the pay scales in the company?</li><li>Are they competitive with other companies in the community/industry?</li><li>How long have the employees been with the company?</li><li>How well-trained are the employees?</li><li>Is there an effective management team in place?</li><li>Will employees and management stay with the company in the event a new owner takes over?</li></ul>These are all questions a potential Buyer will ask. If you can also address these issues, you may be able to implement strategies and procedures that will provide favorable answers to any potential Buyer. This will improve the value of your company.	
Vendor Relationships	<ul><li>Who are your vendors?</li><li>How long have you dealt with them?</li></ul>	

	<ul><li>Do you have contracts with them?</li><li>Are you locked into any particular vendor?</li><li>Are the vendors' prices competitive?</li><li>What are the terms given to your company by the vendors?</li><li>Does your company have any dependency or over-reliance on any key vendors?</li></ul>**If you can improve any situation that may currently be negative, your company value will improve.** Whether positive or negative—document these issues in your business prospectus.	
Governmental/Tax Issues	<ul><li>Are the premises properly zoned?</li><li>Does the company have proper permits and authority to operate?</li><li>Are all products/services properly licensed?</li><li>Is the company in good standing with the Secretary of State?</li><li>Are all taxes paid and current?</li><li>Any pending Tax Audits?</li><li>Any OSHA Problems?</li><li>Any EPA issues?</li></ul>	
Industry Changes	<ul><li>What changes are taking place within your industry?</li><li>What is your company doing to stay abreast of those changes?</li><li>What capital has been spent recently to stay current with industry standards?</li><li>Will material capital expenditures be required in the future to stay competitive within the industry?</li></ul>**Again, by paying attention to these answers now—before you may want/need to sell--you can reduce the actual and perceived risks associated with the industry in which you operate.**	

International, National and Local Economies	• Is the company volatile and tied directly to the global, national or local economies? • Does the company do better in down economic conditions? • Does the company do better in stronger economic conditions? • What can be done to reduce the negative effects of unfavorable economic trends? • Are any of the company's trading partners/customers/vendors adversely affected by differing economic conditions?	
Competition	• Does your company have fierce competition within your market place? • How is your company weaker than your competitors? • How is your company stronger than your competitors? • What can your company do to negate adverse effects caused by effective competition? • What will it cost to overcome the competitive advantages enjoyed by your competitors? • Do you have a plan to fund the costs associated with overcoming the competition's advantages?	

The foregoing risk table gives you some ideas of those areas commonly probed by potential Buyers of your business. If you are prepared to provide honest and positive answers to these risk considerations—you will have enhanced the value of your company.

Checklist: 18 Point Self Assessment Tool

How will the quality and value of your business be perceived by potential Buyers? A good way to anticipate the answer is to place yourself in the Buyer's shoes.

A self assessment tool is provided for your use that will take into consideration 18 common *quality factors* often considered by Business Buyers. This tool will help you see what issues the Buyer might perceive as value. Each factor is scored from zero to four. A zero (0) score indicates the factor adds no perceived value to your business (*carries the highest degree of risk*). A score of four (4) indicates the factor adds the greatest amount of perceived value to your business (*carries a low degree of risk*).

How to use the Assessment: first, critically score each issue as if you were the Buyer. Add together the scores for the 18 quality factors and divide the total by 18. The answer will provide an indication of **perceived quality** of your business. The higher the quality of your business, the higher price your business may bring on the open market. **Example,** if your average score is indicated at 3 or above, your business is in good shape (not perfect…but good). A score of 2 is average, meaning there is room for improvement. A score of less than 2 indicates significantly lower business quality, and accordingly, a much lower anticipated sale price.

On the following pages are two self assessment tools. First is a *completed example* and **the second copy is blank for your use in assessing your own business.**

18 Point Self Assessment Tool: EXAMPLE

Question	Owners Rating	Question	Owners Rating
Profit trends historically are? 0 = going down, 2 = average, 4 = increasing	3.00	**Is operating technology current and up to date?** 0 = major equipment and tech upgrades needed, 4 = technology is all recent	4.00
Income risks-customer concentration, is there heavy reliance on a few customers? 0 = only have one or two customers, 4 = have many customers	2.00	**Is there a reliance on just a few suppliers?** 0 = company relies on hard to replace suppliers, 4 = suppliers are no problem	4.00
Would owner provide any seller financing to buyer? 0 = owner not willing to provide any, 4= offer 30% or more	1.00	**Is there strong competition in your market?** 0 = market is flooded, 4 = strong market position	2.00
Does owner expect business to grow in next 5 years? 0 = owner sees downturn, 2 = small growth, 4 = large growth	3.00	**Can new products be added to enhance revenues?** 0 = you are locked into same service and products, 4 = you are positioned "as is" to expand services	1.00
Owners view of this INDUSTRY growth in next 5 years? 0 = owner sees downturn, 2 = small growth, 4 = large growth	2.00	**Is there a seasoned management team in place?** 0 = you can never get away/no one to take your place, 4 = you take long vacations	0.00
Is current location favorable or unfavorable? 0 = very inconvenient, 4 = extremely convenient to customers	2.00	**How reliant is current business on owner being present to operate?** 0 = very reliant on you to keep production running, 4 = not reliant on you to maintain operations	1.00
Can expansion occur in current location? 0 = need to look for new facility, 4 = room to double (or more) business	0.00	**How easily can licenses/permits be transferred to new owners?** 0 = licenses permits NOT transferable, 4 = licenses and permits easily transferable	4.00
Is business facility in good repair? 0 = in need of extreme facelift, 4 = very useable as is	2.00	**Is your bookkeeping/accounting internally computerized?** 0 =keep records by hand and/or never get recent financial statements, 4 = good technology and financial reporting	4.00
Are non real estate assets in good repair? 0 = need extensive repairs/replacement, 4 = all good for 5+ years	3.00	**Are computer hardware and software systems up to date?** 0 = not up to date (let next owner replace), 4 = all technology is current with most recent upgrades	4.00

Total all Owners Rating Points:

Score = 42.00 **Points**
Divide Score by 18 = 2.3333
Compare answer to Score Key

This example business scores slightly better than average

SCORE KEY

4 – EXCELLENT
3 – GOOD
2 – AVERAGE
1 – NEEDS IMPROVEMENT

18 Point Self Assessment Tool: BLANK

	Owners Rating		Owners Rating
Profit trends historically are? 0 = going down, 2 = average, 4 = increasing		**Is operating technology current and up to date?** 0 = major equipment and tech upgrades needed, 4 = technology is all recent	
Income risks-customer concentration, is there heavy reliance on a few customers? 0 = only have one or two customers, 4 = have many customers		**Is there a reliance on just a few suppliers?** 0 = company relies on hard to replace suppliers, 4 = suppliers are no problem	
Would owner provide any seller financing to buyer? 0 = owner not willing to provide any, 4= offer 30% or more		**Is there strong competition in your market?** 0 = market is flooded, 4 = strong market position	
Does owner expect business to grow in next 5 years? 0 = owner sees downturn, 2 = small growth, 4 = large growth		**Can new products be added to enhance revenues?** 0 = you are locked into same service and products, 4 = you are positioned "as is" to expand services	
Owners view of this INDUSTRY growth in next 5 years? 0 = owner sees downturn, 2 = small growth, 4 = large growth		**Is there a seasoned management team in place?** 0 = you can never get away/no one to take your place, 4 = you take long vacations	
Is current location favorable or unfavorable? 0 = very inconvenient, 4 = extremely convenient to customers		**How reliant is current business on owner being present to operate?** 0 = very reliant on you to keep production running, 4 = not reliant on you to maintain operations	
Can expansion occur in current location? 0 = need to look for new facility, 4 = room to double (or more) business		**How easily can licenses/permits be transferred to new owners?** 0 = licenses permits NOT transferable, 4 = licenses and permits easily transferable	
Is business facility in good repair? 0 = in need of extreme facelift, 4 = very useable as is		**Is your bookkeeping/accounting internally computerized?** 0 = keep records by hand and/or never get recent financial statements, 4 = good technology and financial reporting	
Are non real estate assets in good repair? 0 = need extensive repairs/replacement, 4 = all good for 5+ years		**Are computer hardware and software systems up to date?** 0 = not up to date (let next owner replace), 4 = all technology is current with most recent upgrades	

Total all Owners Rating Points:

Score = _____ Points

Divide Score by 18 =

Compare answer to Score Key

SCORE KEY

4 – EXCELLENT
3 – GOOD
2 – AVERAGE
1 – NEEDS IMPROVEMENT

How to Sell Your Business for the Most Money

Checklist: Mistakes Frequently Made by Business Sellers

1. Business Owners Don't Understand the Buyer's (investor's) Motives

Buyers rely on the past financial results of a company, but only pay for the anticipated future earnings. A Buyer will only pay the Seller for the work the Seller has done in building the business so far, *but will rarely pay for the work the Buyer will have to do to get the business to the next level*. Buyers want to buy a business that has a future and are looking at the future for a return on investment and growth potential after they put their own work into the business.

2. The Owners Assume the Best Investor is Local

Most Sellers naturally assume that the market for their business is the immediate surrounding area. *The world is now your marketplace* and the best investor may be anywhere across the country, or around the world. In addition to the individual Buyer, thousands of very quiet private investment groups and offshore investors are interested in acquiring profitable, U.S.-based, privately-held companies

3. Owners of the Business Don't Understand How to Value Their Business

Most owners of closely-held businesses have suppressed profits to reduce taxes. The company's financial statements don't begin to reflect the true value of the business. The actual financial statements need to be restated to eliminate the owner's discretionary and non-recurring personal expenses. Attention also needs to be drawn to "off-balance sheet assets," tangible and intangible. Historical financial statements don't tell the real story.

4. The Owners Have an Unrealistic Price in Mind

Recent surveys indicate that few companies have a current, accurate business valuation. Often, owners are unrealistically high in their asking price. Whether you think your business is worth $1 million or $50 million, without a professional opinion for reference, you can't begin to discuss or justify a selling price that makes sense to a Buyer.

5. The Owners Don't Receive Proper Counsel

Sellers attempting to take their business to market without professional help are prone to taking advice from the wrong people. Talk with business owners who made an ill-fated attempt to sell their own business. Most wish they had used an experienced Business Broker /Intermediary. Buyers are not that hard to find, but when it's time to make the deal happen, the deal often falls apart without an *experienced business intermediary.*

6. Business Owners Try to Sell to the Wrong People

One of the biggest mistakes is to think that the best investor for the business is a competitor, customer, supplier, or employee. If the deal doesn't happen*, and most don't once it comes down to put the pen to the paper*, then a great deal of confidential information about your company has been disclosed. Suddenly, everybody knows more about the company's profits and operations than they should. Keep your intentions confidential unless you're ready to sell at a rock-bottom price.

7. The Company Is Not Positioned for Sale

Organization, growth opportunity, reputation, market conditions, and industry leadership are some of the many intangible qualities Buyers appreciate and will pay for. Documenting improvements that could be made by a Buyer/investor with new capital helps you to better position the company and increases value. There can be a swing of 50% or more in sale value if the company is solidly positioned for future growth.

8. There is Improper Financial Documentation

Investors are evaluating the purchase of the business based primarily on future growth potential and expected return on investment. Buyers want to see what the profits would have looked like if you had run the business like a public company (*no co-mingling of business and personal expenses*). Often this means recasting the financial statements away from the tax-based accounting that has been done in the past. Buyers also find it helpful to review your three-to-five-year financial projections, backed by solid market research substantiating the future potential of the business. Simply stated . . . create a presentation to explain the past and sell the future!

9. Business Owners Don't Plan for After the Sale

Many business owners have not thought about what their *real* personal financial needs will be after the sale. After debt repayment do you need a large amount of cash for a second home or other investments? If you're willing to wait for a portion of the proceeds (monthly, quarterly, yearly), <u>the Buyer has more flexibility</u> to *pay a higher price*. If you insist on an "all-cash" deal, savvy investors will discount their offering price by up to 35% or more! *Note, this doesn't mean a large percentage of the deal has to be Seller financed; there are ways to guarantee your payments with no risk!*

10. Owners Don't Understand How Taking Tax Deductions Now Affects Future Sale Price

Business owners tend to "write-off" expenses not associated with business activities to save on income taxes. Owners have been known to deduct expenses for things such as vacations, motor coaches, boats, airplanes, farms, personal condos, motorcycles, personal residences, hobbies, etc.. These are expenses that the new owner won't incur and may not be required to operate the business. While trying to be "tax savvy," owners lose sight of the impact such buried expenses may have on their business's value.

> **Insider Tip:** *It's the TAX RETURNS that hold the most weight with the banks and SBA when your Buyer needs loans for acquisition and operating cash. In the couple years leading up to the sale, "clean up" the profit and loss statements and tax returns: pay the taxes, because it is a wise "investment".*

About the Author

Grover "Grove" Rutter has valued and sold numerous businesses nationwide, in a broad array of industries over the past 30 plus years. As a Seller's advocate, he knows what needs to be done to *maximize business value* for his Seller clients.

Mr. Rutter is a *Certified Public Accountant* (CPA), *Accredited Business Valuator* (ABV), and *Certified Valuation Analyst* (CVA), *Business Valuator Accredited in Litigation* (BVAL), a *Certified Business Intermediary* (CBI) and *Master Analyst in Financial Forensics* (MAFF).

While working with retirement and Seller-minded business owners, he became increasingly aware about how little knowledge business owners had concerning business valuation issues associated with their companies. In short, this knowledge is vital if the business owner wishes to convert pre-retirement business income streams into post sale income.

Mr. Rutter is involved in educating business owners and the community about important issues concerning business valuation matters. He has written and presented business and valuation related seminars to various legal, civic, and business associations.

His articles have been published in The Valuation Examiner magazine, The American Journal of Family Law, Valuation Practice Quarterly, Ohio Lawyer Weekly, USA Lawyer Weekly, PatentCafe.com, Bizquest.com, International Business Broker Association's Quarterly, Biz Quest Weekly, Ohio Lawyer Magazine and others.

His first two books, **Your Business IS Your Goldmine** and **How to Sell Your Business for the MOST Money First and Second Edition** earned many favorable reviews and comments from business owners and professionals.

As an experienced *Certified Business Intermediary/Business Broker* and *Certified Business Valuation* expert who is also a *Certified Public Accountant*, he is often hired as an expert witness in legal cases where business valuation issues are in dispute.

Mr. Rutter is a member of the following:

- International Business Brokers Association

- Ohio Business Brokers Association
- The M&A Source
- The National Association of Certified Valuation Analysts
- The American Institute of Certified Public Accountants (AICPA)
- The AICPA Business Valuation and Litigation Support Division
- Rotary International
- Chamber of Commerce

Readers are welcome to contact Mr. Rutter with their specific questions, at grutter@gruttercpas.com . Visit his web site for additional information concerning selling your business at www.gruttercpas.com .

www.ingramcontent.com/pod-product-compliance
Lightning Source LLC
Chambersburg PA
CBHW080934170526
45158CB00008B/2288